"Keep Your Head Up, Mr. Putnam!"

"Keep Your Head Up, Mr. Putnam!"

By PETER PUTNAM

Harper & Brothers . Publishers . New York

CONTENTS

PROLOGUE

In my first attempt to secure a publisher for this manuscript, I wrote a letter to a woman who had been recommended to me as having many contacts in the world of
books. In it, I told her that I had been blinded in a gun
accident shortly before my twenty-first birthday, and that I
had written the story of my experience at the Seeing Eye
school in Morristown some six months later. Very soon
afterward, I received an answer, offering to read my manuscript and expressing interest in "so tragic an experience."
I felt a sinking sensation at this phrase, and when, some
two weeks later, the lady returned my manuscript with the
polite but damning verdict that it was "very well written,"
but "rather slight," I nursed my wounded vanity with the
reflection that she had begun with a misconception and had
been disappointed only because she had been looking for
tragedy. Since that time, I have rewritten my story several
times, and hope I have removed many of the imperfections
which the lady in question was too tactful to point out to
me, but there is still no tragedy in it.

I have no wish to minimize the importance of blindness

as a handicap or to suggest that I myself shrugged it off with a philosophical grin when it fell to my lot. Nevertheless, I should like to point out that the particular circumstances under which I met blindness were nearly ideally calculated to lessen its impact upon me. The bullet which took my sight so nearly took my life that I hovered on the brink of consciousness for days. When my mind had come back to me, and I had recognized my blindness, the sense of returning life was compensation for the loss, and for a long time my bodily weakness forbade activities which demanded the use of my eyes. Then, as my strength returned, I was able to make my adjustments slowly, step by step. After my brush with death, it was like being reborn and learning life all over again, in the dark.

Another advantage was that it was not at first certain that I should remain blind, and it was not until some four months afterward that I had to accept the idea with any finality. By that time I had already learned a good deal and could logically enumerate my other blessings. No one was dependent upon me for a living, and the parents upon whom I was dependent could support the financial burden. No career had been blighted by my affliction, because I had had none, and, in my junior year in college, I had still been unable to form any definite decision as to my future profession. Such notions of the future as I had sometimes entertained were manifestly little more than the daydreams of aging adolescence, and two activities for which I had long had a hankering were still open to me. These were teaching and writing, and I might never have had the courage to try them if I had kept my eyesight. I had a wonderful family to help me over the bumps. I had my health. I had a reasonably active mind. I had a life expectancy of some fifty years, and I had a will to live it. All I had lost was my eyesight.

That is the bright side of the picture, but convalescence, like adolescence, has its ugly as well as its beautiful side, and blindness demands a fairly long convalescence. I experienced many tensions, irritations, and frustrations, and I can vividly recall many moments which fill me with shame. I was still convalescing when I went to the Seeing Eye, and my convalescence did not end there. Perhaps I am convalescing still. I did not enter the place as a broken reed and leave it as a tower of strength. But, at the Seeing Eye, there was gradually unfolded to me the vision of the world in which I would henceforth live. I have tried to tell the story of that experience, not as it might have been, but just as it was. It was a great experience. Nothing about it was tragic.

"Keep Your Head Up,
Mr. Putnam!"

CHAPTER I

The Unexpected

CLONGG! . . . CLONGG! . . . CLONGG! . . . CLONGG! . . .
The metal reinforcements of my heels rang on the pavement. My cheeks quivered with each jarring impact, the muscles of my knees and thighs felt stiff and wooden, and my shins sent forth little aching tremors at every step. Despite the chill of the autumn morning, I was perspiring freely, and the raw skin of my left hand rubbed painfully against the harness handle of a Seeing Eye dog, tugging me along the street at the rate of nearly four miles an hour. Before me lay a block almost half a mile long, a downgrade all the way, and I knew I would encounter uneven surfaces made slippery by the patches of half-frozen moisture which lay here and there in the hollows of the pavement. Nevertheless, I felt an unreasoning lightness of heart as I pounded along that morning in 1941, and I

smiled continually at nothing as I drew in the breath of late fall air.

Behind me some ten or fifteen paces, a fellow student at the Seeing Eye school in Morristown, Mr. Bauermann, was being hauled along in a similar fashion, while, bringing up the rear in rubber-soled silence, came the third member of our convoy, our instructor, Mr. Northrup. In the point of physical discomfort, I knew I had the better of Mr. Bauermann. In his middle thirties, he was some fifteen years older than I, and his two hundred and thirty pounds had already taken a cruel toll of his feet in the ten days we had been navigating about the streets of Morristown. For three successive nights, he had heaved his great bulk upon the bed to remove his shoes, groaning the same lines: "Hits not the 'eavy 'aulin' what 'urts the 'orses' 'oofs. Hits the 'ammer, 'ammer on the 'ard 'ighway." We had all, including Mr. Bauermann, considered this a great joke, and now, as we marched along, its humor leavened my own discomfort, for I knew that Mr. Bauermann's dog, excited by an atavistic herd instinct, would be pulling doubly hard to overtake mine. " 'Ammer, 'ammer, 'ammer" was right. Our feet, supporting some four hundred pounds of sweating humanity and propelled forward by two eagerly straining dogs, struck the sloping pavement in unison, with an impact which echoed on the still air in the otherwise deserted street like the sound of a crack Prussian regiment demonstrating the goose step. At the thought of Mr. Bauermann's pulsating arches, my smile broadened, but it was not alone this innocent malice which explained the source of my inward elation.

* * *

Three weeks before and less than forty miles away, walking down another street in another town, I had been feeling a similarly unreasoning elation. The street was Prospect, the town was Princeton, and the excitement which surrounded and warmed me on all sides was that of a gala college football Saturday two hours before game time. Everything around me was familiar. The shoulder on which my left hand rested belonged to Dick Sayer, a boy who had been my roommate since prep school, and I could remember the shade and pattern of his Harris tweed, pleasantly rough under my palm, because I had helped him pick it out less than a year ago, when we had both been juniors. With us were Ben Williamson, another former roommate, and Ann Wylie, a girl whom I had met less than an hour before, but so very like a dozen other girls I had known on such football weekends that our relationship was already automatic.

I had walked down this same street hundreds of times, and so, even though I had not been here for six months, I knew just how it must look. I pictured to myself the avenue of trees with the neatly kept borders and lawns and the solid brick and stone façades of the upper-class eating clubs set back on either side of the walk which stretched away before us. Mentally I recited their names: Dial Lodge, Colonial, Tiger Inn, and Elm, on our left, and Campus, Tower, Cannon, Quadrangle, Ivy, Cottage, and Cap and Gown, on our right. Cottage had been my club, and it was peculiarly important to me that it was still my club as we walked toward it now.

More than half consciously, I was experiencing a strong sense of my identification with the crowd which thronged the walk before and behind us. I felt it with the under-graduates, dressed like me in tailored suits, white shirts with button-down collars, and conservative small-figured ties, strolling along with lazy confident strides, looking and feeling as if they owned the place. For the most part, I knew, they would be wearing neither hats nor overcoats, for they were confident even of the bright fall afternoon, and this was a confidence I shared, for, after all, I was still one of them.

I felt it with the girls beside them, chatting, laughing, or just looking animated and pretty, wearing suits or hats or matching alligator shoes and purses which they had, perhaps, bought specially for this occasion. Pinned to their lapels would be yellow chrysanthemums, tied with the colors of Princeton, and that was still my college. I felt it with the alumni, ruddy and jovial in their serviceabl_ tweed overcoats and battered felt hats with orange souvenir feathers in them, but faintly harassed, too, with the steamer rugs and thermoses of coffee they carried, as they shepherded their wives and, occasionally, their children along the crowded path. I had six living relatives in the Princeton alumni body, and I was sure that some of these men must have been among their classmates. And I felt it even with the children, for, years before, I had myself walked along with the crowd, feeling strangely constricted about the neck by my clumsily knotted tie. In years to come, I might find myself here again with a child of my own, a leggy girl, perhaps, primly self-conscious in her unaccustomed high heels and wondering whether the seams of her new silk stockings needed straightening. This egocentric basking in the warmth of group belonging was suddenly interrupted by the energetic shouts of a young man on our left.

"Get your Fanny-ette early!" he chanted hoarsely. "Genuine foam rubber! . . . Turns a concrete seat into a horse-hair chair! . . . With a Fanny-ette, you'll never want to stand in the stands!"

I had forgotten how the venders contrived these absurd singsongs, made purposely ridiculous in order to prick the attention of the holiday crowd, and I laughed, suddenly remembering again how it was and how it would be. The

· 5 ·

souvenir mongers would raise the pitch and tempo of their voices ever higher until just before game time. The hurrying crowd would spill over the walk onto the gravel surfaces which lined it, and a few impatient undergraduates would break into a run along its fringes. People would shout hurried greetings and repeat instructions as to where to meet after the game. The sunlight, pouring down through the thinning branches and the translucent yellow leaves which floated, here and there, overhead, would dance in the shining hair of laughing girls and over the fur scarves of the women and through the orange feathers bobbing along far ahead under the perspective of the trees.

Then, suddenly, the whole wave of humanity would wash over the street, leaving only a faint rustling tremor in its wake: the rapid echoing footsteps of a few stragglers, the bang of the big front door of one of the clubs, shuddering away quickly into silence, and the muffled voice of the stadium loud-speaker, ghostlike in the distance. Standing amid the cigarette butts and mustard-stained paper napkins littering the cement and gravel surfaces of the walk, an old man would patiently rearrange the little souvenir tigers and footballs on his display board and plod off after the crowd, leaving the yellow leaves to float softly down through the still clear liquid of the late fall air hovering tremulously in the empty street. That was how it would be, and the conviction of this certain knowledge further buoyed my feeling of kinship with the festive crowd as we strolled along.

*   *   *

We turned off the walk to the right, and Dick's voice cut through my connections with the impersonal crowd and brought me instantly back into contact with my friends.

"Where are we now, Pete?" he asked.

"Easy," I said. "The University Cottage Club." I removed my hand from his shoulder, handed him my cane, and performed a low salaam. They all laughed.

"How'd you know?" Ann asked. "I didn't."

"The brick walk," I kicked my heel against its surface, "portends the 'Brick Shack.' "

"The 'Brick Shack'?"

"The name," I explained, "which the unlettered sometimes apply to the elegant pile before us." Ann laughed cheerfully at almost anything, so I pointed my cane and went on, very pleased with my own success. "Note the classic simplicity of the Georgian style and the geometric effect of the white marble quoins setting off the . . ."

"Cut it out!" Ben said. "I get enough of that stuff in Art 306."

"He's not really blind," Ann said. "He's faking."

"I'm dodging the draft," I said, pleased again. "Once

I get a Seeing Eye dog to replace this cane, my disguise will be impenetrable."

"Slacker!" Dick said. "Look out, now! We're coming to the door."

Inside, the clamor of voices engulfed us. As we threaded our way through the standing crowd, there was a shout of "Hi, Pete!" from across the room. I smiled and shouted back, but I did not recognize the voice, and we were headed in the opposite direction.

"Let go of Dick," Ben said, "and give me your other hand."

I did as I was told, and he pulled me through.

"God, what a crush!" I said, "and, boy, how I love it!"

"Here we go," Ben said. "Down these steps."

"Where are you taking me? Don't lock me in the cellar. I want to stay with all the pretty girls."

"All the pretty girls are right behind you," Ann said.

"The alumni had a bar put in the basement this summer," Dick explained. "Wait'll you see it. It's very classy. We're meeting Sandy down there."

I followed Ben down the stairs. We turned left, walked a few paces, and turned again down a longer flight of stairs. At the bottom, we turned right, and I could tell by the sudden contractions of the echoes that we were going through a door. There were many people sitting in this new room, and as we walked, I twisted my body sideways with each rotation of Ben's shoulder to avoid the crowded tables and chairs. I was grateful to Ben for our swift sure passage across the room.

"Hey, group!" Ben called.

The answering shouts came, I guessed, from a table in front of us. I recognized the boys' voices, and I was introduced to two new girls.

"Here's a chair," Dick said, pushing it behind my knees so that I nearly fell into it.

"Easy does it!" I said and reached to my breast pocket for a cigarette. That was something I had gotten into the habit of doing as soon as I came into a new room. It furnished a protective screen of action, behind which I could take my bearings and listen to the relative position of people's voices without seeming to do so. Sandy Prentiss, one of the strange girls and Ben Williamson were on my left. Ann Wylie, Dick Sayer and Dave Compton were on my right. The rest, I decided, were too far away to matter, but I felt a renewed tingle of excitement at the thought that I was back among them.

"Here!" Sandy took my hand and put a drink in it. "Force a little bourbon down your throat."

"Thanks," I said. I took a long drink and settled back as Dick launched into an enthusiastic description of the new bar.

That was how it began, and it seemed like a very fine

beginning. We finished our drinks and had another. We talked and laughed in shouts above the clatter of the room, and our conversation was all what we used to call "the old cheap chatter." Dave Compton insisted on taking me up to the bar to test the rail, and when I put my foot on it and called, "Look Ma, no hands," everybody laughed. Everybody laughed at everything. For a while, I rode with the crest of my exhilaration at being back, and the warmth of the whiskey, and the social distinction my blindness gave me, but, then, without any warning, the wave passed over my head and left me floating in its receding wake. I felt tired, removed, a little ashamed of the flush on my face, and, as the remembered sound of my own voice rang in my ears, I was suddenly convinced that my part in the cheap chatter had been really cheap. I had been subject to such emotional oscillations since my blindness and should have been able to guard against them, but Prospect, the club, the girls, the whiskey, and the old friends had been too much for me after the months of absence. I would have to slow down, and I was glad I had arranged to stay in the club instead of going to the game.

"Drink up, everybody!" Dave Compton called. "Let's get this show on the road. If we don't get upstairs and grab some lunch, we'll be late for the kickoff."

"You children toddle on ahead and get your roughage,"

Sandy said. "Pete and I are going to have another drink. We never eat on an empty stomach."

"Are you sure you wouldn't rather go to the game?" I asked. "You don't have to stay with me, you know. I'd be fine by myself."

"I'd rather hear it on the radio," Sandy said. "I'm too nearsighted to see anything anyway."

Dick was standing behind my chair.

"We could still get you a ticket if you'd rather go," he said.

"No, this is fine," I said. "I'm kind of tired. I'll meet you here afterward."

We lingered in the empty bar for a while after the others had gone, and then Sandy took me upstairs, through the deserted hall and out onto the terrace court. A lone waiter was noisily piling plates and glasses upon a metal tray. The surface warmth of the sun on my face gave me the feeling of the brightness of the day. Sandy led me forward across the terrace to a comfortably cushioned cane sofa, and I sat down while he went back inside to get us each a plate from the buffet. The leatherette of the cushions was warm against my legs and back. Behind me, in the court, a trickle of water splashed in the little stone fountain where goldfish were sometimes kept in the spring. Ahead of me, down the slope of the hill, the muffled voice of the loud-speaker announced the pertinent statistics of each play, and the occasional roars of the crowd wavered up to me on the soft breath of the cool wind. A fly lit on the back of my hand, making a tiny spot of cold. Dreamily, I pondered this for a moment. Maybe the fly's body was itself cold, or, maybe, even in those few square millimeters of shadow, the absence of the sun was noticeable on the surface of my skin. I slapped and was pleased to feel it, for an instant, under my fingers at the moment of contact, and I remembered, then, that flies got sluggish and easy to kill in the fall. Sandy came out on the terrace behind me.

"I just killed my first fly in six months," I said.

"Good," Sandy said. "Glad to see you keeping yourself amused. Here's food."

He set down the plates on a coffee table in front of us. I was hungry, and I ate with concentration. There was some tomato aspic that kept falling off my fork, and I was glad there was nobody but Sandy there to see. I felt relaxed and secure there on the terrace, and I was ready to suggest that Sandy turn on the living-room radio loud enough so that we could hear it without moving, but he spoke first.

"Dick tells me you're planning to get a Seeing Eye dog."

"That's right."

"Does that mean there's no more hope for your eyes?"

"I suppose there's always hope for a miracle," I said. "The bullet hardly touched my eyes at all, but the optic nerves are pretty well shot. I don't even have light perception. If there were anything left of the nerves, there should have been some sign of it long ago."

"That's tough."

"I'm lucky I didn't get killed." He seemed a little embarrassed, so I went on. "Here. Give me your digit. I want to show you something." I took his forefinger and guided it to a spot on my left temple. "Feel that?"

"What is it?" he asked, poking gingerly at the hard little node under the skin.

"That's the bullet." I had to laugh at the way he jerked his hand away. "It didn't quite get out the other side. The doctor says it's better to leave it there than to risk infection in an operation."

"Well, I'll be darned," Sandy said, and then added, half under his breath, "A gen-u-wine lead head."

Sandy's earthiness was a refreshing change from the studied and sober tactfulness I had come to expect from older people, and I laughed, but he had taken up the thread again.

"How soon will you get the dog?"

"I don't know," I said. "My mother's picking me up in the car tomorrow. We're spending the night with my grandfather in New York, and we'll drive over to Morristown on Monday. We arranged it this morning after the interview with the Dean."

"The Dean?" I was sure from the way Sandy asked that he hadn't heard.

"Yes," I said. "My mother and I went in to see him this morning as soon as we got down. If I can get a dog, I'm all set to come back next February."

"Are you kidding?"

"I'm not kidding. Why would I be kidding?" I was a little miffed at Sandy's surprise, but I kept smiling.

"Aren't you rushing things a little?"

"What did you expect?" I asked.

"Well, I don't know." Sandy's voice had become deprecatory and reasonable, and I guessed he must have been thinking about it and, maybe, talking it over with some of the other boys. "I don't know much about it," he said, "but I understand that they have blind schools where you could learn various techniques and be with other blind people. . . ."

"For God's sake, Sandy," I interrupted. My voice echoed in the courtyard. "Take it easy. You're just like all the rest. The minute you're blind, everyone wants to reclassify you, put you in a separate group, in a separate niche. That looks like Peter Putnam, they say, but it couldn't be, because this guy is blind. Put him with the blind people. What in the world have I got in common with the other blind people? Except my blindness. Why not put all the people with false teeth together? Or blue eyes? Or . . ."

"Calm down," Sandy said. "I'm not trying to classify you, but you could learn the various techniques. . . ."

"Various techniques! What various techniques? Making brooms? Weaving baskets?" Then, I stopped. "Sorry, Sandy, I didn't mean to blow up. I really don't know anything about blind schools either, but, actually, I don't see what's in it for me. I'm sure not very many blind people go through college, and I don't see what they could teach me that would help me get a Princeton degree."

"There's Braille, isn't there?"

"I should have told you about that before spouting off. I'm already learning it. It's the kind of thing you have to teach yourself. A state teacher came to the house this summer and showed me the main principles, and since then, I've been practicing with a primer. I'm not very good, but I'd only use it for lecture notes anyhow."

"What about the assignments?" Sandy asked.

"Braille would be too slow for them, even for an expert, and it would probably be darn hard to get them in Braille. I told the Dean I'd pay boys in the same courses to read aloud to me. They shouldn't be too expensive, because it's reading they'd have to do anyway. With the honor system, I could take exams in another room on a typewriter. I can type pretty well by the touch system."

"Well, you seem to have it all figured out," Sandy said,

mollified, but still dubious. "I just hope you're not biting off more than you can chew."

"Time will tell," I said, "but just look at the alternatives. I'd go crazy spending a year in a school with a bunch of blind jerks. It will be bad enough at the Seeing Eye for a month. Besides, if I waited until next year to come back, all my classmates would be graduated, and I wouldn't have any real friends. There's another angle, too. If I don't get going pretty soon, it will confuse things with my family."

"How's that?" Sandy asked.

"Well, my father's in the regular army. He was all set to retire, and that's why he bought the farm in Litchfield, when he was stationed in Hartford. Now, what with the peacetime draft and the threat of war, he's decided to stay in, and he's been ordered out to Fort Riley, Kansas. It's so crowded, there's only room for my mother in his quarters. My sister's out of the way, because she's married, and my brother's away at The Hill School, but if I couldn't come back, my mother would have to stay with me in Litchfield."

"Well," Sandy said. "If you're just doing this from family pressure . . ."

"Nuts!" I said. "There isn't any family pressure. I've got to get back. After moving around in the army all my life, Princeton seems more like home than any place else."

"You win," Sandy said. He sounded a little weary of the subject. "Why don't I get us a drink, and we can toast your future success?"

"Fine!" I said. "And turn on the radio while you're at it."

* * *

As he went for the drinks, I had another unpleasant vision of myself, haranguing Sandy excitably with flushed face and quick nervous little gestures. What was the good of making speeches. My vehemence could seem only a sign of an inner instability. I had pressed my surface reasons for coming back with so much heat only because I had not dared to attempt an explanation of my secret inner urge, and I was grateful I had not. I could never have explained it, because I did not understand it, and, even now, ten years later, it is difficult to understand. How is it possible to explain a reaction so contrary to the dictates of common sense? There was nothing in it which I could have expected.

At some time during the ten days of semidelirium in the hospital, I had become conscious of the fact that I was blind, but I cannot remember the moment or nature of that discovery. Nor because of a brain concussion and drugs and, perhaps, a natural instinct to suppress the remembrance of pain, can I remember much in the way of physical discomfort. What I can remember is a totally unexpected and largely unaccountable sense of exhilaration. I had not, I think, been particularly afraid of death, but I had been afraid of life. I should say, rather, that I had been afraid of my own life, or, better still, of the consequences to me of the seemingly inevitable failure of a life which, throughout adolescence, had been haunted by the gnawing suspicion that it had no central core of will or purpose. What surprised and exhilarated me, as I returned to consciousness, was not so much that I was alive, but that I was so terribly glad to be alive. I felt reborn, and the curious thing about this sense of resurgent life was that it took the form of a physical sensation so strong as to be almost tangible.

I can smile at the romanticism of the simile now, but, at the time, I compared the life fever stirring in my bones with what a tree must feel in the spring sap rising from its roots. I had, I felt, an organic center, and that organic center had not been touched, or, quite the contrary, it had been touched, but only to be brought into self-realization. The future, including future blindness, seemed a challenge to which I was now wholly committed, and this challenge transformed my view of the world. Graduation from Princeton, a meaningless formality toward which I had been stumbling with half a heart, now seemed the very symbol of my first step toward this new world, and I no longer felt the old adolescent fear of failure. In short, I wanted to live as I had never wanted to live before.

* * *

The afternoon and the evening whirled by with the old familiar excitement of all the football Saturdays I had ever known at Princeton. After the game, there was a drink or two at the club, a party in one of the dormitory rooms, a dozen oysters and a steak sandwich at the Nassau Tavern, followed by beer, pretzels, and singing, and, finally, a long taxi ride for a midnight snack and a final drink at what had been a roadhouse speakeasy during the days of prohibition. It was all wonderful, but, the next morning, lying on the day-bed in Dick's and Ben's room, what I most remembered were snatches of my thoughts and conversation on the terrace.

Seen in the sober light of the morning, I began to realize that my whole focus had been onesided. I had thought and spoken only of my confidence and had admitted none of my anxiety. I had emphasized all my convictions and none of my misgivings. Now, these began to grow upon me with a force which obscured all real recollection of the next twenty-four hours. I know that my mother drove down from New York to pick me up in the car. I know that we nosed steadily through the Sunday traffic back to my grandfather's house on Riverside Drive. I know that we had dinner and spent the night there and that the next day, after an early lunch, we again set out in the car for Morristown. But, until we pulled into the drive before the Seeing Eye, I can recall clearly nothing except the private thoughts revolving through my head, and even these shared in that lack of substance which is the common denominator of all anxiety.

I knew of this anxiety only that it was inseparably connected with my feelings about the Seeing Eye. From the moment, several months before, when the idea of obtaining a dog had first been suggested to me, I had felt a certain distaste for the place. I had been reluctant to believe in the permanence of my blindness and shrank from accepting so public and concrete a badge of handicap as a cripple might shrink from the first sight of a corrective shoe. In recalling a lecture given by Morris Frank, the owner of the first Seeing Eye dog, when I had been a student at The Hill School, I remembered, not the gay and confident presence of Mr. Frank, but the posters which had heralded his appearance. Drawn by the art students, they depicted blind men and women being led by their dogs in a style which combined adolescent literalism with the motionless unreality of an Egyptian tomb fresco. My vanity was grated by the mere thought of identifying myself with those stiffened profiles.

The very name, Seeing Eye, seemed both redundant and

silly. The first letter had brought a prying questionnaire and the information that each applicant must be prepared to spend a minimum of four weeks in the training course at the school in a class with seven other "blind jerks," as I had termed them to Sandy. If I could return to Princeton, I would know what to expect. I could visualize in detail every walk, every building, and, very nearly, every class-room I would be called upon to enter. I had many friends among the students and acquaintances on the faculty, and in that sense I had not been exaggerating when I told Sandy that, more than any other place I knew, Princeton was my home. But to return to Princeton I had first to undergo the unknown, for, despite all the preparation and correspondence, the Seeing Eye had no reality for me. There I would have to take everything that came my way sight unseen.

Once arrived at the school, it was no longer possible to doubt its reality. It was an eminently substantial Victorian structure, but, as we sat stolidly in the waiting room, listening to the echoing sounds from the upper floors of the old building, I felt suddenly like a small boy about to meet the principal of a new school. Somewhere across the hall, a typewriter bell punctuated the intermittent clatter of the keys, and the drone of a vacuum cleaner buzzed in my ears like the sound of taking ether.

A few moments later, we were ushered into the office of

a Mrs. Campbell, an elderly lady who received us with a gracious, almost courtly reserve. The closing of the door shut out the vacuum cleaner and I felt better, but Mrs. Campbell began almost immediately to review with us verbally the matter of our earlier correspondence. Somewhat nervously, I outlined my situation. I would find no difficulty in meeting the absurdly low tuition fee of one hundred and fifty dollars, the only payment required from a student in return for a dog and a full course of training with board and lodging at the school. I did not, at that moment, have with me a note from my doctor certifying my physical fitness, but assumed that, since I had been up and about for several months, this would be only a formality. Most important, I emphasized the urgency for haste since my readmittance to Princeton the following February had been made conditional upon my possession of a Seeing Eye dog at that time. My reasoning gathered momentum in the face of her courteous condescension, and I talked more than I had meant to.

"I think I may have good news for you, Mr. Putnam," she said, when I had finished. "We've heard of a cancellation in the class beginning next Sunday, and we may have a spot for you there." My mother and I exchanged murmurs of surprise, but it appeared they were still premature, for Mrs. Campbell had not finished. "I've sent for one of our instructors, Mr. Myrose. He's going to take you outside to test your co-ordination." She rose and walked toward to the door. "No, Mr. Putnam, you wait here," she said as I got up to follow her, and she went out without closing the door behind her.

"Gee, it looks good," I said to my mother with a smile and a confidence I did not feel.

Mr. Myrose, when Mrs. Campbell had introduced him, shook hands and said he was glad to meet us, but he wasted no time in formalities. "All right, Mr. Putnam," he said. "I'm going to take you out for a little test. Take my elbow, we're using a different door than the one you came in."

He led me out, down a short cement walk and onto a gravel surface, where he stopped and placed a rigid U-shaped handle, covered with leather, in my left hand. It was like the ones the dogs wore attached to their harnesses, he told me, and he was going to lead me around with it. I held onto my end of the handle while he walked ahead over the gravel at what seemed an extraordinarily rapid pace, changing his direction suddenly to the right and to the left. After about a dozen such gyrations, he asked me to point toward the house. I aimed a hesitant finger, and we followed its general direction back to the entrance. Inside, I rejoined my mother in the waiting room, while Mr. Myrose conferred with Mrs. Campbell in her office. In a few minutes, she emerged.

"You seem to have passed your examination, Mr.

Putnam," she said in a smiling tone. "We'll have room for you next Sunday, if you can make the necessary arrangements. Are there any questions you would like to ask?"

For all my impatience for decision, the interview had taken place with a speed which was breathtaking after the slow-moving months of isolation. I could think of little to say except thanks. I remember I asked her whether I could bring a portable phonograph and some records.

"I'm afraid not," she answered with polite finality. "Your roommates may not be music lovers, and anyway, Mr. Putnam, you'll be too busy with your dog to allow much time for other distractions."

We thanked Mrs. Campbell and Mr. Myrose and left. When we had gotten in the car, my mother spoke for both of us.

"It doesn't leave us much time, does it," she said. "But, anyway, it's a decision, and it's a step in the right direction."

"Yes," I said.

"It's too bad you can't have your records."

"Oh, well. . . . They've got to be careful about those things," I patronized, but inwardly I chafed.

That was that, I thought. My suspicions had been borne out. Everything about the place had a cold and uncompromising air. It would provide a bleak contrast to my Princeton weekend. Still, it would be only a month—a month, that is, unless, I thought with a sinking sensation, I did not prove an apt pupil. But that was silly. A month, I repeated, and a month was a very short time, considered in the light of what lay beyond it. I would have to suppress my normal reactions, my conversation, and even my thoughts as an individual, but the nomadic existence of a regular army officer's son had equipped me for that, surely. It would be like taking a long swim under water. The figure struck me as a good one, and I pursued its implications. You filled your lungs with the air of your native element. I had done that at Princeton. Then, you took the plunge, and it was important not to think about your lungs, or it would be worse. Just concentrate on keeping your arms and legs working. That was it. It would be simply a form of suspended animation. Like bacteria in a hostile environment, I would combat the spiritual chill of the Seeing Eye by assuming the form of a spore.

That was what I had expected, and the memory of this expectation flashed through my mind on that morning, three weeks later, as I pounded along ahead of Mr. Bauermann, sweating from the physical exertion. This was certainly nothing like suspended animation, and, as I filled my lungs with the fresh fall air, I was glad I was not under water. And that was the real reason for the smile on my face that morning.

CHAPTER II

Juno and Minerva

ABOUT THREE O'CLOCK IN THE AFTERNOON ON THE Sunday following the interview, equipped with "waterproof raincoat," "stout walking shoes," "warm clothing allowing for ample freedom of movement," and a sense of misgiving, we rolled into the driveway in front of the Seeing Eye. I was unloading my bags from the rear of the station wagon, when footsteps approached over the gravel.

"How do you do, Mrs. Putnam," a cheery voice greeted. "I'm Mr. Northrup. I'm the instructor for the class your son is in. Well, Mr. Putnam, I see you've brought plenty of clothes with you."

This remark was aimed at the size of a suitcase which my mother had given me as a school graduation present, and, in truth, it was a monumental piece of luggage.

I hoisted it quickly as a good-will gesture, while we shook hands. Then I groped for the other bag.

"I've got the little bag and the typewriter all right," Mr. Northrup said, "if you can manage that trunk. Follow me."

"You must be awfully busy on this first day," my mother said, as we started up the driveway.

"Today, I am ubiquitous." He pronounced the last word rather proudly, as if it were something he had been saving for an occasion, and then proceeded with a running fire of conversation which continued until we had reached my room. "There are six steps up to the porch, Mr. Putnam— Don't help him, Mrs. Putnam—and then three paces to the storm door. This way . . . the inner door opens to the left . . . and, now, across the hall to the stairs. You'll be on the second floor. Let him do it himself, Mrs. Putnam. There's a column at the end of the banister you can use to find the railing." He slapped the column ahead of me. "There are twelve steps to the first landing . . . another column . . . ninety degree left . . . six steps . . . column . . . landing . . . left again . . . six more steps . . . and the second floor. Got it?"

I nodded and followed as he led the way up the steps, slapping railings and columns.

"I went to college myself . . . Duke . . . where they play football . . . I understand they've heard of the game at Princeton." He laughed. It had been a season which Princetonians would have been only too happy to forget, while

Duke men looked forward eagerly to a bid to the Rose Bowl.

"We invented the game," I said.

"Just a slip of the memory yesterday, I guess," he answered. "Well, here we are on the second floor. Your room's down to the left, and then the first door to the right. You'll have two roommates, but they haven't arrived yet. Here's the door. . . . No, a little more to your left. . . . It's all right, Mrs. Putnam." I entered the room and put the huge suitcase down.

"Now, this is your bed, and this is the bureau right next to it, and . . . over here is the community closet." He pounded each in turn, and, not knowing what to do, I followed suit and pounded them, too. This ceremonial tattoo concluded, he led me across the hall to show me the lavatory and ended by ushering us both into the Recreation Room. We had no sooner entered than a hail from below called him away to greet another student. When he had left, my mother and I eddied uncertainly for a moment in the wake of the conversational whirlwind.

"He seems *very* nice," my mother said.

"He certainly is hearty."

"Well," my mother said, "maybe we'd better unpack your things."

"Oh, I can do that after you leave. It's the sort of thing you have to do yourself." I was unconsciously adopting that attitude of remoteness common to boys at boarding school toward their parents. "Let's have a cigarette."

We sat down and talked for a few minutes. The chairs had wooden frames and broad wooden arms, but comfortably upholstered backs and cushions.

"It just seems crazy for me to be going all the way out to Kansas," my mother blurted out impulsively. "Are you sure you'll be all right?"

"Sure," I said. "It's only a month, and, now that Poppa's leave is certain, we know we'll all be together on the farm for a big Christmas. Besides, you couldn't visit me except on Sundays anyway."

"I think that's just silly," my mother said. "They don't have to get so dramatic about it."

We both laughed, because we both knew that we had quite resigned ourselves to the letter of the law, as laid down by the Seeing Eye. Dozens of times before, we had conformed similarly to the impersonal blanket regulations of schools, college, and a variety of annoying exactions attendant upon army life, but it was characteristic, in the very act of acceptance, to register some such token protest amongst ourselves. It made us feel more intimate, more aware of a sort of family conspiracy to outwit the domination of bureaucratic red tape. I was temporarily warmed by it, but, in a moment, I was thinking that if I were to take this underwater plunge it would not do to think about my lungs.

"I don't know how much time I'll have to write," I warned her. "Don't worry if you don't hear from me too often."

"No, I won't," my mother reassured. "And you can always get anything you want by calling up Plainfield. Don't forget, it's 6-2515." This was the number of my uncle's house in nearby Plainfield, where he lived with his daughter, a few years older than myself.

"Don't worry," I said. "I've called it so often I know it in my sleep."

"I saw a phone right outside the room here. On the right. On the wall between here and your bedroom. It's a pay phone."

"Fine," I said.

"Call me up Tuesday night when I get to Riley, just so I'll know everything's O.K."

"I promise," I said. "But don't call me. I don't know when I'll be free. And don't worry if I sound formal. I'll probably be harry."

This last was a family signal. My parents had invented it during their engagement to explain the presence of possible eavesdroppers close to the telephone. Again, I had to remind myself not to conjure up these personal associations. They were disturbing to the mental program I had

outlined. When my mother, divining my mood, got up
to leave, I accompanied her downstairs and stood at the
top of the porch steps as she drove away. Then I went back
inside and across the hall, groping rather awkwardly for
the banister.

"Keep your head up, Mr. Putnam, and stand up
straight!" Mr. Northrup called from the top of the stairs.
I jerked back my head, which I had allowed to creep forward, apelike, in reaching out for the railing.

"I'm sorry," I said foolishly.

"It's all right," he assured me. "It's a frequent mannerism of the new blind, but it's a good thing to catch early,"
and he bounded on up the stairs. He certainly was hearty!

* * *

The memory of my first hours at the Seeing Eye is as
devoid of color as a mist. I unpacked slowly, arranging
linen, socks, sweaters, and accessories methodically in the
large sheet-metal bureau, and hanging suits and coats on
wire hangers on one side of the closet I was to share with
my roommates. There was a small wooden table by my
bed, on which I placed my typewriter. I had, as yet, nothing about which to write a letter. I decided, instead, to
explore my surroundings without the embarrassing presence of spectators. I felt out the position of the windows
and of my absent roommates' beds and bureaus. In one
corner, there was a fireplace with an old-fashioned mantel-

piece, decorated with what I took to be Grecian floral designs. Touching it, I stood lost for a moment suddenly reminded of the big mantels in my grandfather's house on Riverside Drive.

My grandfather's mantels had been much bigger, elaborate mahogany ornaments with applied columns and pilasters in the classic style. I had played in front of them as far back as I could remember, fascinated by the gas logs that burned perpetually without being consumed all through a cold winter's day. I had been startled on seeing them, midway through an architecture course in college, to find how many details I had missed before. The columns were capped with garlanded Ionic capitals, supporting an architrave bordered with egg and dart moldings and fronted with a row of rosettes. I thought of the architecture course and tried to remember the parts of the Doric order. Three steps . . . What were they called? Then, plinth, fluted shaft, proportioned at six to one in the Parthenon colonnade, echinus, abacus . . . What were those three little lines around the necking of the column? Then, architrave, triglyphs, metopes, pediment, and cornice. I remembered that the columns were slightly tapered and curved to heighten the perspective. Diminution and entasis, that was called. Those were good words. They compensated for the other things I had forgotten, and, half aloud, I rolled them over my tongue, feeling better.

The sound startled me, and I was irritated at myself for this woolgathering. I was forgetting. I was supposed to be under water. I turned back to the wall, feeling my way toward the door. I crossed the hall to the lavatory, where I opened the wrong door and almost plunged headlong down a back staircase. In the Recreation Room, I found eight chairs like the one I had sat in, a piano, a radio, a number of standing ash trays, and a large wooden table off to one side. In a far corner there was a bookcase with several magazines in Braille type which I found undecipherable. This reminded me of my remarks to Sandy, and, as there seemed nothing else to do, I decided to bring my new Braille primer into the Recreation Room for a little "recreation" until something else turned up.

I sat down in one of the big armchairs, lighted a cigarette, and began to puzzle at the little combinations of dots in the unwieldy cardboard primer sprawled on my lap. The first page contained the symbols for the first five letters of the alphabet and words made up of them. There are only a limited number of words which can be constructed from these letters. "Bad," "bed," "cab," the primer spelled out slowly, "bead" and "babe" were next. "Dead," it interjected ominously; "a bad babe," it admonished, and then, as if to distribute the blame, "a bad dad." The climax to this tedious family tableau came when "dad bade a bad babe abed." It occurred to me that the substitution of the colloquial for the domestic meaning of the word "babe" might imply a rather questionable state of affairs and corroborate the former verdict of "a bad dad," but I was not particularly amused. I could make out the characters only with difficulty, and the unnecessary muscular tension of overconcentration quickly tired my wrist. I paused frequently to rest it, smoking and listening to the stirrings downstairs and in the hall. All the floors were covered with linoleum, as I later learned, to minimize the effect of occasional "accidents" by the dogs, and they echoed with an unpleasant institutional sound.

On two or three occasions, passers-by paused on the threshold of the room for a moment. I looked up questioningly and smiled, but when I said nothing, they went on their way. It never occurred to me that these swift and sure footsteps could belong, not to members of the staff, but to my blind classmates. Even when one of them, hearing me cough, introduced himself as Ted Ballard, shook hands, and sat down to talk, I did not for some time recognize him as a fellow student and, as it turned out, one of my roommates. In any case, my introduction to Ted Ballard and one or two others had little meaning for me at the time, and the passage of the years has quite obscured its details in my mind. In the previous months of relative confinement, I had become unaccustomed to meeting new people, and under the weight of the depressed anxiety which I felt on that first day my concern was less for the personalities of these strangers than for the specific problems of a new physical environment. I was less interested in human relations than in the physical proportions, shapes, and positions of the concrete objects of my surroundings.

Our first meal together did little to dispel this diffidence toward my classmates. About six o'clock, Mr. Northrup mustered the full membership of eight at the top of the stairs in the hall and explained to us the route to the dining room. There was a slight delay before the actual descent to permit the members of the other class to precede us. Their apartments connected to the stairwell from a wing on the other side. Having arrived two weeks earlier, they were already at an advanced stage of the course, and I later learned that to avoid unnecessary distraction to their dogs, we were never supposed to visit with them. I listened to their footsteps, their unintelligible commands, and the jingling chain collars of their dogs with all the mixture of uneasiness and envy of a draftee on his first day in an induction center watching a disciplined regiment entraining for a trip to actual combat. When the last of them had gone down, we descended in single file at regulated intervals, pausing to feel of steps, columns, and doorways under Mr. Northrup's supervision, so as to fix the way in our minds.

In the dining room, he arranged us all behind our chairs around a long table near the door. The veteran troops, I gathered, were deployed at smaller tables to the right of the entrance. Then, Mr. Northrup gave the signal for the class to take their seats and it was not until that moment that we were all formally introduced.

I retained clearly only one of the new names: that of Mr. Curtiss, a quiet young man of about thirty, who sat on my left, and whose identity was worthy of remembrance because he was to be my other roommate. There were six men and two women in all, and I was mildly interested to discover that they hailed from places as widely separated as Chicago, St. Louis, Washington, and Boston, in addition to some small towns with which I was unfamiliar. The five other men had had dogs before, it appeared, and they inquired after former classmates and various members of the Seeing Eye staff, but the talk as a whole was desultory, and only the conversational energy of Mr. Northrup prevented a total lapse. I listened for the most part, trying to distinguish the different voices, and concentrating on eating as neatly as possible.

After supper, Mr. Northrup conducted us back upstairs. He told us that we would be expected to assemble in the Recreation Room at eight for a little talk. I went to my room for my Braille slate, so that I might attempt a few "lecture notes," and hurried back to the Recreation Room.

Mr. Curtiss' support enabled me to dominate the radio controls long enough to hear the Jack Benny program, and when it was over, I felt better. We talked together until Mr. Northrup came in with another member of the staff whom he introduced as Mr. Humphrey, the vice-president in charge of training. I put my Braille slate in readiness, but it soon became apparent that I would have no use for it, as Mr. Humphrey, speaking in low, level tones, confined himself to outlining the school's house rules. Some of these were routine, others were incongruous, and all were faintly depressing. Meals were to be served at 7:30, 12:30, and 6:00, respectively. Gentlemen were expected to attend in coats and ties; ladies, in dresses or skirts, not slacks or shorts. Ladies and gentlemen were not to fraternize in each other's quarters. There was to be no smoking in bed or possession of liquor. To avoid any semblance of favoritism, there would be no use of first names between students and staff members. Cigarettes, candy, or other supplies could be purchased through Mr. Northrup by speaking to him directly after breakfast each day. It was all made perfectly clear, and there were not, as I remember, any questions.

I did not feel much like sitting around the Recreation Room when Mr. Humphrey had finished, and, in a few minutes, I left to undress for bed. It felt strange to have to wear a bathrobe to cross the hall to the lavatory. This time, I found the right door and avoided the back stairs. When I got into bed, I could hear the voice of Walter Winchell from the radio close to my head on the other side of the wall in the Recreation Room. I felt tired and empty, and when Mr. Curtiss and Mr. Ballard came in from the other room, I pretended to be asleep. They were still moving about, conversing in whispers, when I dropped off.

* * *

On the following morning, we entered upon a preliminary program of education designed to prepare us for the eventual introduction of dog to master. It lasted only two and a half days, but it seemed an endless interim, and it scarcely demanded that strenuous effort of concentration I had been taught to expect. The general level of monotony was broken by only two forms of activity. One of these was sedentary and consisted of listening to little "lectures" by Mr. Humphrey and Mr. Northrup in the Recreation Room. Mr. Humphrey described the historical background of the Seeing Eye school: its roots in Switzerland, the impetus given to its foundation in America by the training of Morris Frank's famous Buddy, its early infancy in Nashville, and its final establishment, only ten years before, in its present home in Morristown. We were told, too, of the general qualifications of our dogs as guides, such as their natural ability, with either eye or ear, to determine the exact speed of a moving object, and these were illustrated by concrete examples. More specifically, it was explained how dog and master cooperate in their work, how the dog stops at all curbs, intersections, and obstacles, how the master then gives the required command of right, left, or forward, and what intonation of voice and movement of hand and body must accompany each command. All this was interesting, even fascinating, but it interrupted the general tedium for only the smallest fraction of each day.

The other aspect of our preparatory training was more immediately satisfying. Each morning and afternoon, Mr. Northrup, dividing the class into shifts of four each, drove first one, and then the other, quartet of students into Morristown, three miles away. I remember being pleased to find that the car was a Ford station wagon like my Mother's. Once parked, Mr. Northrup took us one at a time from the car and led us about the streets by a harness handle, similar to the one Mr. Myrose had used the week before, in a practical application of the instructions we had been given in the lectures. We used the code name "Juno" to address the symbolic canine whose part was conscientiously played by the eminently human Mr. Northrup. In these sample perambulations, he emitted no sound, but padded along slightly ahead and to the left, stopping at all curbs and crossings, and wheeling to the left or to the right in response to our commands and accompanying gestures. His self-effacement gave me a sense of independence, and, after a preliminary hesitancy, I learned to stride along rapidly with body and head erect, overcoming the "frequent mannerism of the new blind."

Mr. Northrup, it developed, had a genuine penchant for pantomime and seemed to enjoy these walks as much as we did. Looking back, I suspect his pleasure was marred only by the fact that our inexperience would not permit him to play his role to the hilt, stopping, perhaps, to sniff a crumpled candy wrapper in the gutter, or swerving to make acquaintance with a passing mongrel. "Juno, forward!" "Juno, right!" "Juno, sit!" we would command, and as the response was unvarying obedience, it was always incumbent upon us to add, in tones of simulated rapture, "Atta *good* girl, Juno!" This act of reward was the first principle of all guide-dog work, and I was anxious to do my duty conscientiously; nevertheless, the element of the ludicrous in these honeyed endearments to the enthusiastic football fan from Duke never failed to strain my dramatic credulity.

These brief excursions were virtually the only activity in a long day devoted to waiting. After breakfast, we waited, either upstairs, or on the porch for the station wagon to drive us to Morristown. In the station wagon, three of us waited our turns, while Mr. Northrup led the fourth around the streets. Back at the Seeing Eye, four of us waited, either privately or in the Recreation Room, for the other half of the class to return, and when they had, the entire class waited for lunch. In the afternoon, the same tedious process was repeated, and, after dinner, having waited for a talk from Mr. Northrup or Mr. Humphrey, we sat in the Recreation Room, talking or listening to the radio, waiting until it was time to go to bed. It was not until the third day that I discovered really what we had all been waiting for.

*   *   *

On the morning of the first Wednesday, Mr. Northrup gave each of us a typewritten sheet. From mine, he read aloud the following data:

Name:	Minnie
Sex:	Bitch, Spayed
Date of Birth:	April 23, 1940
Weight:	59 lbs.
Color:	Fawn

The name, Minnie, seemed to me to reflect a singular lack of inspiration on someone's part, and I decided, privately, to call her Minerva, but, Minnie or Minerva, I looked forward eagerly to the meeting to take place that afternoon. Mr. Northrup kept us in a tantalizing suspense throughout lunch and refused teasingly to set the exact time of our introduction. Finally when we had all finished eating, he pushed back his chair and announced: "All right, class. When you get upstairs, you will each go to your own room, shut the door, and wait until I call for you."

Upstairs, the waiting began again. Mr. Curtiss, Mr. Ballard, and I sat in our room, smoking, and trying to talk naturally. Twice we paused to listen to the sounds of a classmate walking down the hall with his dog. Then, more rapid footsteps approached, the door opened, and Mr. Northrup's voice called out: "Your turn, Mr. Curtiss. Come and get her!"

I lit another cigarette and leaned back in my chair. I had begun a second before the door opened again. Mr. Curtiss was speaking baby talk in a low tone, not to some mythical Juno, but to a living reality, whose claws scratched the floor, whose breath came in excited pants, and whose chain collar jingled musically, as he walked her toward his bed.

"You're up next, Mr. Putnam," Mr. Curtiss said. "Mr. Northrup's waiting for you in the Recreation Room." The zero hour had at last struck.

"Over here, Mr. Putnam," Mr. Northrup said, when I had reached the Recreation Room. He slapped the back of one of the big armchairs farthest from the door. I walked over and sat down in it. He gave me a leash and, guiding my hands over its length, explained its design to me. It had metal clips at both ends and could be used in two ways: either "on short leash," when it was doubled in half by snapping one end to a ring at the other extremity, or "on long leash," by snapping this same end to another ring much higher up, where it made a convenient loop for the master's hand. For this meeting, Mr. Northrup explained, it would be used at long leash.

"When I bring her in, she'll run over to you. I'll give you a piece of meat to give her with your left hand, while you fasten the leash to her collar with your right. Then, you hold the loop in your right hand, and grab the leash with your left about twelve inches from the collar, like this, and take her back to your room at heel. She'll pull at the leash, and it'll pay big dividends if you jerk her back hard right at the start. Your command is 'Heel! Minnie, heel!' . . . and, if she pulls ahead, big jerk with the left hand. . . . 'Minnie, atta *good* girl!' . . . Understand?"

I repeated his instructions with an earnestness which apparently amused him. "Go to the head of the class," he laughed. "Now, when you get her back to the room, make a big fuss over her. She loves to be played with, and you've got to make her like you. Remember, she's the most important woman in your life right now. . . . O.K.? . . . Take it easy now."

With this parting reassurance, he pressed a piece of ground meat about the size of a golf ball into my left hand and hurried off to fetch Minnie from the kennels in back of the house. I listened to his jaunty footsteps descending the stairs and the final echoing bang of the big front door. The house seemed strangely silent. The closest I had ever come to such a sensation before was backstage, during those last few minutes before curtain time in the Princeton Triangle show. I wanted to smoke, but didn't know how long I had to wait, and I would need both hands when Minnie came. Several minutes ticked by before the door slammed again. Mr. Northrup was talking to Minnie as they came up the stairs together. I don't remember what he said, but I can never forget the sound of Minnie's claws slipping on the linoleum. She came through the door with a rush, and I extended my hand with the meat cupped in it, but she was not interested in that. She was half in my lap, wiggling all over, snuffling at my clothes, and licking my face and hands. It was a long half minute before I could give her the meat. While she ate it, I snapped on the leash and started for the door. Minnie tugged ahead, as Mr. Northrup had predicted, and I attempted a couple of jerks on the leash, but they were largely ineffectual. I felt very strange.

At the door of my room, Mr. Northrup put his hand on

my shoulder, bending toward me. "O.K., Mr. Putnam, be good to her. She's a beautiful blonde bitch," he said in my ear, "perfectly suited to a Princeton man."

That was my first meeting with Minnie.

* * *

From that time on, the Seeing Eye assumed a new complexion, but the change was not immediately apparent. At first, it was necessary to keep all the dogs on "bedchain." This was a chain strung upon a piece of wire underneath the bed and bisecting it laterally. There being three in the room, the dogs could not be allowed to roam at will. In the excitement of their new surroundings, any playful roughhouse might culminate in a fight. To permit them time to acclimatize themselves slowly, we were forbidden to take them into the Recreation Room, and, to avoid offending their sensitive nostrils, were even advised not to smoke for the first days. Except for meals and other necessary business, we were to stay with our dogs in our rooms and to make friends by playing with them.

To Minnie, the words "play" and "bite" were entirely synonymous. Whenever I advanced my hand toward her head, moving cautiously so as not to stick a finger in her eye, she would nip it painfully, and as I hastily snatched it away again, she would dart after it in an ecstasy of delight. It was utterly impossible to stroke or to feel of her. For over an hour after our first meeting, I knew no more of "the most important woman in my life" than her teeth, which, from incisor to molar, appeared to possess the most admirable occlusion. I had imagined the relationship of the Seeing Eye dog to its master as the sort of thing pictured in the dog stories of Jack London or Albert Payson Terhune: a devoted loyalty tempered by a dignified aloofness. I had half wondered whether Minnie would expect me to spend long winter evenings by the fireside with slippers and pipe, and whereas I was relieved to be excused from so incongruous a role, I found the attempt to befriend a dental whirlwind no less trying. When I snapped on the leash for the descent to supper, however, her mood instantly changed. She behaved perfectly on the trip downstairs, pausing at the edge of each landing and sitting there obediently upon command. She lay quietly at my feet throughout the meal, and that night, after Mr. Northrup had taken her for an airing, she subsided completely. As I climbed into bed, Minnie set to work on the little rag rug provided for each dog, shaping it into a nest with her forepaws. I reached out and felt her shoulders working, her head bent forward, her ears pointing up straight in concentration on the problem. She was too absorbed to bite my hand.

"Atta *good* girl, Minnie!" I said in the rapturous accents with which I had learned to address Juno. She paused for a moment and looked up. Her bushy tail, striking against the sheet metal of the bureau by my bed, made a pleasant low booming sound.

*   *   *

After breakfast the next morning, the second phase of the course at the Seeing Eye was definitely launched. Speaking from the head of the long table, Mr. Northrup included my name among those who would go to Morristown on the first shift, and, as soon as he had supervised the ascent of the stairs, he came to the room to oversee the harnessing of Minnie. Thus far, we had moved about with our dogs on leash only. Since Minnie was still in a highly volatile state, I had anticipated that this might prove a rather delicate maneuver, but I had scarcely presented the harness in position before her, when she wiggled herself into it eagerly and began to lave my face with a generous tongue. Indeed, such was her enthusiasm for her work that she never failed of this same response whenever I took the harness in my hands either during the course or throughout her later life.

I took Minnie downstairs at heel and put her at sit at the top of the porch steps to wait with three other classmates for Mr. Northrup in the station wagon. When it came, we clambered in one at a time according to his directions. The master went first, leaving his dog at sit on the porch, backing down the stairs to the open door of the waiting station wagon. He held the palm of his right hand outward as if pushing it toward the dog; at the same time, he repeated in a calm, quiet voice the words "Juno, rest," calling her only when he had seated himself inside, whereupon she followed with a joyous rush to sit between his knees on the floor. The whole procedure was designed to curb the dogs' eagerness for automobile riding, for experience had taught the staff that, without it, these enthusiastic motorists would have dived indiscriminately through the open door of any strange car.

Four men and four large dogs were crowded into the two back seats of the Ford station wagon, but no one complained of discomfort. When we had arrived in town, Mr. Northrup took us singly over the prescribed route for the morning. I was not first, but the wait seemed not unpleasant, because, for the first time, we really had something to talk about. Like children comparing Christmas presents, we described to each other the names, ages, weights, and colors of our dogs.

When my turn came, I stood in the middle of the sidewalk while Mr. Northrup explained it all to me again.

"Put your dog at sit on short leash. . . . That's it. . . . Now, you'll hold the leash in the middle and ring fingers of your left hand and curl the four fingers around the harness handle. . . . No, not yet! Wait till I tell you. . . . Don't grip with the thumb. You want a loose grip with the wrist held back. The forward pull of the dog will keep the harness handle in your hand without gripping tightly. . . . If you should lose the handle for any reason, you'll still have your dog by the leash held in your two fingers." He paused, and I nodded.

"All right. Put your dog at sit again." I told Minnie to sit. She had gotten up when Mr. Northrup had moved back.

"Reward your dog, Mr. Putnam!" came sharply from Mr. Northrup. In my impatience to be off, I had forgotten to congratulate Minnie for her obedience to the command of sit.

"Atta *good* girl, Minnie!" I cooed.

"All set. . . . 'Juno, forward!' . . . whenever you're ready."

I picked up the harness handle as he had told me, and Minnie started forward immediately without waiting for my command. I followed her rapid lead and had gone several paces before I remembered to reward her with my voice. It seemed to me an entirely new form of locomotion, like skating, bicycling, riding, or skiing, or, rather, like the first uncertain sense of mastery of them with the heightened awareness that comes of novelty. We had rehearsed with Mr. Northrup at about the same rate of speed, but this was quite different. With him, there had been something mechanical, prearranged, and artificial in our movements. Now the harness handle was vibrant, pulsating with the smooth oscillations of Minnie's shoulders. It was both more graceful and more awkward. It was more like being a freestanding and freely moving body. I found myself smiling with a sort of blushing shyness I had not known for a long time.

Minnie stopped suddenly, and we were at a curb.

"Atta *good* girl, Minerva," I said. I put out my right foot to feel for the edge.

"Minnie, sit!" I elongated the last word, drawing it out with an upward inflection, while gently lowering my left hand, still grasping the leash and harness handle, against her rump, as Mr. Northrup had showed me. I was somehow amazed and grateful at the promptness of her response. I felt the same warmth that one feels flowing from a circus audience at the goodness and the docility of waltzing elephants.

"Atta *good* girl, Minerva!" I said, but I was not a mere circus spectator, and my mind hummed with concentration upon my instructions. There was absolutely no room for fear, and when we crossed the street, I walked boldly toward the sound of a lone car passing in front of us. It was like that all through the first walk. The physical activity, the mental preoccupation, the warmth of gratitude, the sense of novelty and independence possessed me entirely, and I lost track of the number of blocks and turns on the quiet street, feeling quite alone with myself and Minnie. I was startled when Mr. Northrup called from some distance behind me.

"All right, Mr. Putnam. Drop your harness handle, and lead her back to me at heel."

I turned and walked toward his voice, some twenty or thirty paces distant.

"We always have the dogs walk past the station wagon for a little way, so that they won't get the idea of returning to it mechanically over a fixed route," he explained as I came up to him. "Give her a good pat, now. Well, how'd you like it?"

"It was wonderful," I said. "An amazing sensation."

"I always get a big kick out of watching a new student take his first walk," he said, "no matter how many times I've seen it before."

The warmth in his voice swelled the slow elation I felt rising within me, and I stood smiling at him for a moment in the bright morning air before I got back into the station wagon.

CHAPTER III

The Human Comedy

DURING THE VERY EARLY DAYS AT THE SEEING EYE, I formed but a dim impression of my seven classmates. At first, they were only voices in the Recreation Room which I did not identify, footsteps in the corridor which I sought to avoid, elbows at the dining table which I tried not to bump. Later, being thrown so much in their society, I could not help making further observations and even enjoying them, but my attitude remained for some time distant. I was eager to get along with them, of course, but our connection was, after all, only temporary, and I began to be interested in them, not as individuals, but as representative social types whom I had not previously encountered. A further difficulty was the fact that our contact, although often annoyingly close, was periodically interrupted by the demands of the course, and, even now, my recollections of my classmates are largely limited to a number of episodes,

· 52 ·

strung along on the routine of our existence like beads on a wire.

Socially, the day began in the Park. This euphemism designated a large rectangular plot of gravel behind the house where we took our dogs for the performance of their natural functions four times daily: before breakfast, lunch, dinner, and bedtime. The trip down the stairs and over the cement sidewalk demanded the main focus of our attention, but, once arrived in the Park, where we removed the dogs' harnesses and allowed them the limited freedom of long leash, we were able to take more notice of each other as individuals. The fall put real snap in the air, and it was chilly in the Park at six-thirty in the morning. Mr. Torbak and Mr. McNeill, the senior members of the class, were the only ones who didn't seem to mind it, and, although the one was a Pole from Boston, and the other a Scotsman from Chicago, they were thrown together as roommates and used to joke about each other's snoring, while the rest of us shivered in silence.

Mr. Torbak's Pilot was the only male dog in the class and was nearly always the first to "do his duty" in the morning. As with everything else, this demanded a vocal commendation from the master, and Mr. Torbak, if unlearned in some of the niceties of English diction, was more than eloquent in his praise. In stentorian tones, he would rumble his approval, and his "Bilutt, detsh a goot poy!" splitting the chill atmosphere, always signalized for me the start of each new day.

There was a large boulder on one side of the Park to serve as a sort of point of departure for the trip back to the big house. Unlike myself, Mr. Torbak never seemed to have any difficulty in locating this landmark, but, once having found it and replaced Pilot in his harness, he was at a loss for his direction. I should say that he had a surfeit of directions, for Torbak was made of that stuff which is never at a loss. Aiming himself at any one of a half-dozen points on the horizon, he would emit a Napoleonic bellow, "Bilutt, vorwarts!" and off he would careen into the unknown, until Mr. Northrup set him to rights.

As I gradually relaxed within the framework of the routine, I began to distinguish the personalities and backgrounds of my seven classmates. The long waits in the station wagon, the return to the Recreation Room, when the dogs had begun to accustom themselves to their new surroundings, and, later, when the need for Mr. Northrup's immediate supervision was no longer constant, the happier custom of eating at small tables in groups of two or three offered many opportunities for conversation. Mr. Torbak and I were several times marooned together in the station wagon during the early days, and it was by this means that I first learned something of his background. He was currently employed as the concessionaire of a small stand at which he sold magazines, candy, and soft drinks, but he told me that, before his blindness, he had a "pig chop" in the municipal waterworks in Boston.

"I mekk fiftinn tousan' tollars a year," he mused meditatively. "It wuss pig chop."

Apparently, however, even this prosperity had not deterred him from a foolish economy. He had developed cataracts in both eyes and, contrary to what is now standard procedure, had undergone operations for both simultaneously. A twin surgical failure had cost him his eyesight, but, despite his handicap, he had managed to do well for his family. One of his sons was preparing for a medical career, and the other was a student at a nationally famous academy of music. Perhaps the high regard for the value of education which this reflected accounted for the paternal exhortations with which he used frequently to address me. I had told him that I would first use Minnie to help me complete my undergraduate course at Princeton, and it was a decision which he heartily approved, but which he seemed somehow to fear I would ultimately revoke. Thus, he would frequently urge me on to my college studies, as if the plan were an entirely new one.

Upon entering the Recreation Room, he invariably took the seat nearest the door and just as invariably, regardless of time or circumstance, barged into the conversation with the same demand: "Gat sum noose on de radio!"

A Pole and a Jew, he had an insatiable desire to follow the course of the war, but seemed not to know how to operate the radio controls. After a few minutes, alternately listening and growling under his breath, he would suddenly rouse himself from his black torpor.

"Mr. Bottnum!" he would shout.

"Yes, Mr. Torbak?" I would answer.

"You yunk! . . . Go to Brinnston! . . . Stoddy. . . . Gat adjucashun. Detch goot, my Got!" And without waiting for my reassurances, he would rise and stump out of the room with Pilot.

* * *

Mr. McNeill, Mr. Torbak's contemporary and roommate, rather fancied himself as a wit and enjoyed twitting his friend about one thing and another. As a practicing Jew, Mr. Torbak regularly received packages of kosher delicacies from his family in Boston, and Mr. McNeill publicly threatened to steal some for his dog, unless "Tobaccy," as he called Mr. Torbak, would offer to share it.

"I got it hid," Mr. Torbak would answer with sturdy complacency.

"I know where, too, Tobaccy—on the floor of your closet. I'll just open up the door and tell Martha [Mr. McNeill's dog] 'Fetch!' I'll tell her, and then it won't be my fault. 'I never touched your baloney, Tobaccy,' I'll say." The Scottish Machiavelli became ecstatic in expounding this legal ruse, but Mr. Torbak was ready with an answer.

"Vot's de matter, McNeill?" he rumbled. "You got Jewish dug, huh?"

The two roommates fought to a similar verbal draw on the subject of baseball. Mr. Torbak, it seemed, was a loyal fan of the Brooklyn Dodgers, but recently vanquished by the New York Yankees in the World Series of that year.

"You ought to be for the Braves or the Red Sox, Tobaccy," Mr. McNeill argued, "You're from Boston."

The reply was a mere grunt, but, when Mr. McNeill had taunted him with certain humiliating details of the World Series fiasco, Mr. Torbak was stung into a reply.

"I like de Dotchers. Dey blay brave." And, in truth, there could be little quarrel with this resolute justification.

* * *

Mr. McNeill was full of little jokes or, as they might more properly be called, "wheezes." If these were not uproariously funny, they seldom passed the bounds of strictest propriety; nevertheless, an exception was fated to disturb his relations with one of his classmates. In order to indulge his joy as a raconteur, he hoarded his little stories, telling them to only one student at a time, so that he might go the whole round of the class. The story in question, a fair sample of his brand of humor, was told to me in the washroom one evening in the midst of a shave before dinner.

"It seems there were two charwomen in London." Here, there was a touch on my arm, and I lowered my razor. "An' one of 'em says, 'Ain't it awful these air raids we're 'avin', dearie?'" The touch on the arm became a grip on the elbow. "'Yes,' says the other, 'we're liable to be blasted right into maternity.'"

I laughed uncertainly on the assumption that this was the punch line and was about to return to my shaving, when a tightened grip on my elbow arrested me.

"'And what with these confounded blackouts,' says the first, 'we won't know 'oo done it!'"

In his innocence, Mr. McNeill committed the social blunder of telling this little joke to Mrs. Clay, a widow in her middle forties from St. Louis and a modest and unassuming woman in everything which did not concern her rather aggressive sense of respectability. She promptly informed him that she was not accustomed to hearing such stories from gentlemen, although, as Mr. McNeill indignantly commented, "She didn't say what she was accustomed to hearin' from the ladies!" She actually went so far as to request that she not be compelled to eat at the same table with Mr. McNeill in the future. Mr. Northrup quietly arranged for her transfer and, further to calm the teapot tempest, assigned the antagonists to separate shifts in the station wagon for several days after the incident.

* * *

The calm surface of student relations was more violently disturbed several days later in a clash involving the re-doubtable Mr. Torbak and one of my roommates, Mr. Ballard. The latter was a young man of twenty-six from a town near Pittsburgh, and, for reasons I cannot account for, I had formed a distinct mental picture of him as a large, florid, and rather fatty young man with straight sandy hair and a gold tooth. He had a high reedy voice, and I imagined his expression to be attentive, eager, or shy, by turns, but nearly always smiling. His first act, after the preliminaries of our introduction, was to show me a tie clasp presented to him for the trip "by the girls and boys at the country club." He made me feel of it, while he launched into a detailed pictorial description in which I felt keenly the elements of both the incongruous and the pathetic, since its visual aspect could hold but an academic interest for either of us. He told me he owned a large record collection and a portable loud-speaker which he took to various dances and entertainments in his home town, and it was in this capacity that he had met the group who had given him the tie clasp. Apparently, the pay derived from these services was his only independent source of income, and, for the rest, he cooked and kept house for a widowed mother who worked in a department store. Years of sheltered solitude had made him rather old-maidish, but it was impossible not to wish to encourage his eager sociability.

He had had a dog before, and I often asked him questions about the potentialities and limitations of a guide dog. Would I be able to take my dog to the movies? What about revolving doors, escalators, or subways? He was always archly evasive at first, because those who had had dogs before had been warned to give no instructions to the novices. In the past, such instructions had often proved ill-timed, inarticulate, and misleading, but I could not see how the admission that he had taken his dog to the movies could possibly injure my work with Minnie and would ultimately bring him around. Despite his seeming coyness, he proved to be only too anxious to offer advice, and it was this, in combination with an unfortunate strain of sententiousness, which proved his undoing in his relations with Mr. Torbak.

I was writing letters in my room one morning when Mr. Ballard returned from the second trip to Morristown. He seemed agitated in reply to my greeting, and my curiosity was piqued.

"What's the matter?" I asked. "Did something go wrong?"

He was reluctant to speak at first, and I had to press him with further questions.

"Oh, that Torbak!" he fumed. His a's, when he spoke, were flattened to the sound of a sheep's bleat. "That d-a-a-mn Torb-a-a-k!" he bleated.

"What did he do?" The use of profanity was far out of character for Mr. Ballard, and my interest was further whetted.

"I was just trying to help him. He wasn't making Pilot sit at the curbs, and just 'cause I tell him, he goes and gets m-a-a-d at me."

I had a clear mental picture of him, then, pouting with lowered head, shifting his weight from one foot to the other and fussing with the adjustment of his prized tie clasp. Before I could say anything to soothe him, however, Mr. Torbak's voice startled us from the doorway.

"Look, you yunk punk!" he shouted. "*You* dunt tal *me* vot to do! . . . Detsh for Mr. Norttrupp!" His voice rose, and his words jumbled together, so that I was not sure that he was still speaking English. He paused, breathless for a moment, then bellowed. "You kip your gottam nose outta my gottam bisniss, alse it gat ponched!"

"We'll see about th-a-a-t," retorted Mr. Ballard, flustered, but with a show of bravado.

"I vorn you!" Mr. Torbak threatened. "Stay de hal outta my bisniss! . . . Mr. Norttrupp . . . he tals me . . . not *you,*

you yunk punk! . . . . Alse you gat ponched de gottam noss!"

Mr. Ballard, mad and a little scared, said again that they would see about that, but Mr. Torbak had already left the field of combat, and when Mr. Northrup arrived a few minutes later with the feed pans for the dogs, there were no signs of the recent conflict. In any case, as Mr. Torbak and Mr. Ballard were already assigned to separate dining tables, there was little need for official intervention.

* * *

I had been amused and secretly comforted by such foibles in my fellow students, for they seemed to demonstrate weaknesses which I myself did not possess and furnished a sense of superiority as an overlay to my basic insecurity. My laughter was satiric, based upon values which, I felt, the actors in the comedy did not understand, and which, therefore, I could not share with them. But, as the course progressed, I became aware of another sort of humor, common to us all, and based on a sense of camaraderie which took me quite unawares. The fact was that, above and beyond a passive sense of unity, imposed from outside by our mere physical proximity, we were all individually activated by an ambition toward a common goal. As I became increasingly aware of this, I found that our varying successes and failures engendered a common sympathy, because, irrespective of differences in background and temperament, we all found ourselves confronted with the same basic problems.

There were, indeed, a great variety of these problems. To begin with, the mere act of following a guide who tugged along at four miles an hour often taxed both muscular co-ordination and physical strength, and none of us escaped some measure of soreness and stiffness from this unaccustomed physical exercise. The memorizing of the order of commands and the rewarding of every act of obedience or intelligent disobedience had to be made second nature, and our praise must never seem to the dogs merely perfunctory, no matter how trying the circumstances in which we were required to utter it. It was difficult, notwithstanding every conscious desire, to regulate our instinctive reactions in accordance with the signals transmitted to us through our guides' harness handles, and these signals were not always easy to interpret. For example, it was difficult to know, when a dog veered suddenly, whether the maneuver had been designed to avoid an oncoming pedestrian or merely to sniff up an acquaintance with a neighborhood mongrel. In the first instance, it was requisite that the dog be praised with the perpetual "Atta *good* girl," and in the second, that she be reprimanded with "Hopp, hopp!" a phrase borrowed from the German and roughly equivalent to "Pay attention to business."

As we progressed, the routes became increasingly difficult, and we were exposed to every species of problem which the streets of Morristown could afford. These included an active downtown business area, intersections which came in, not at right angles, but at deceptive diagonals, cracked and broken sidewalks with trees jutting into them, a park with curving paths and distracting squirrels, and a repaving project, where we had to contend with improvised detours off the sidewalk and the nerve-wracking staccato of pneumatic drills. Amid all these perils, our daily odysseys through the streets of Morristown were often far from the pleasant jaunt I had experienced with Minnie on that first day, but they served as the catalyst which fused the discordant elements of our individual personalities into a tight social compound.

For my part, that which aggravated all other difficulties was the necessity of memorizing the itinerary of our daily route and subsequently directing Minnie over the prescribed course. Contrary to a still widely held misconception, the master of a Seeing Eye dog does not, like the fare of a taxicab, simply give the address of his destination and then give up his mind to other preoccupations until his arrival. His dog, to be sure, guides him around obstacles, up and down curbs and steps, and through moving traffic, but it is he who must select the streets and walks over which they travel, and in a strange city burdened with nervous concentration upon a dozen other concerns, this was often a difficult assignment. Before each trip, Mr. Northrup described our route to us, listing the names of the streets, the number of blocks, and the sequence of the turns. Accuracy of memory meant everything. To confuse "Cross and turn right" with "Turn right and cross" was easily done, but the consequence of such a mistake was disastrous, for it placed the student upon the wrong side of the street, and since the number of intersections upon one side of the street often failed to correspond with those on the other, error begat error until the confusion was abject and entire. The student might stop to inquire his whereabouts of a passing pedestrian but unless he exactly remembered the names of the streets (and one of these changed three times in as many blocks), the answer failed to clarify his position.

Mr. Northrup, of course, was in constant attendance, but he conducted his convoys in silence in order to simulate actual conditions, so that we learned to rely upon ourselves and, to a limited extent, upon whatever assistance we could give each other. This latter was made possible by the fact that we traveled in pairs and, in so doing, stopped at curbs to wait for each other, both in order to alternate the lead and to prevent a separation too wide to make Mr. Northrup's supervision practicable. These curb stops were often the scene of hurried conferences between students as to their probable whereabouts and next destination. They were always a comfort as a temporary relief from the sense of total isolation; they were frequently useful in preventing future errors; and, in one instance at least, they were even the means of snatching victory from defeat in one of those bizarre mischances which lay in wait for us in the middle of the block. The instance referred to illustrates the way in which our common difficulties could forge for us a bridge of sympathy between widely divergent personalities.

It occurred on an occasion when Mrs. Clay and Mr. McNeill, still on terms of tacit hostility, were paired together for a walk through a residential area. Mr. McNeill had been in the lead and, having arrived at the end of a long block, waited patiently for his partner to come up, until at last, irritated and a little concerned at the long delay, he reversed his direction to go in search of her. The deserted block should have offered no problems for an experienced hand, but Mrs. Clay was a novice, and as ill luck would have it, she and Vera had encountered a cat on their way. Even then there would have been no difficulty, had not Vera's startled movement deranged her mistress's still uncertain orientation. As a result, she had directed her unwilling guide off the sidewalk, down a flagstone path, and onto a tennis court, where, with the exception of the small gateway by which she had entered, her exit was barred by a high wire netting. Having scuffled about in confusion for several moments, she had been reduced to nervous immobility from which Mr. Northrup, who had been looking on with silent interest at a situation which strikingly paralleled "actual conditions," was about to rescue her, when the gallant McNeill suddenly appeared. Having successfully directed Martha to the sound of Mrs. Clay's stationary muttering, he, too, entered the snare, but found himself no better able to cope with the situation. The two held a brief consultation, and then Mr. McNeill began to grope about the meshing of their athletic prison. There was quite an interval before the light finally dawned, and Mr. McNeill began to shake with laughter.

"Do ye know what we've wandered into now, Mrs. Clay?" he asked in tones of one reciting a riddle.

"I certainly do not!" said Mrs. Clay, annoyed at being left out of the secret.

"It's a tennis court. That's what it is, a tennis court!" he announced with triumphant emphasis, and then burst out: "I wonder now, Mrs. Clay, did ye bring yer racket with ye?"

The words became a catch phrase among the students of the little class, and Mrs. Clay, doubtless experiencing again her sense of relief at first hearing them, always led the laughter. Indeed, I fancy she saw something romantic in her mutual captivity with her former enemy and used to tell and retell the story of the little adventure with a lack of restraint which surpassed even that of her co-prisoner with his tale of the London charwomen.

* * *

At some time during the course, every member of the class was paired off with every other, but my own most frequent companion in the streets of Morristown was the only person in the class younger than myself, a girl of nineteen from a small town somewhere in Tennessee. Her name was Miss Burke, but from the time that Mr. Northrup discovered at the dinner table that she had twin cousins actually baptized with the incredible names of Militia Dixie and Bookedge, respectively, I, clever wag that I was, used always to call her Militia or simply Milish. Her only rejoinder, in this instance, was to retaliate by addressing me as Bookedge, but the real quality of her humor lay in her manner of speech, which, for color and emphasis, was the rival of any I have ever heard. Her most amusing idiosyncrasy was the habit of interjecting the words "Bad off!" or "Worried!" into the frequent anecdotes of her personal history, as an indication of her condition or emotional state at the moment she was describing. Her words would run together quickly and then come to a sliding stop in the jerky, graceful rhythms of a good open-field runner in football, changing his pace to avoid would-be tacklers.

"Me'n' Paig wuz crawssin' up bah the buhss depot, when

this grea'-big-ole-truck [all in one breath] chuhgged bay
and splaished muhd'n wateh all o'vah mah shews. . . . Bad
off! . . ." Here Milish paused to elude a tackler, but she
soon gathered speed in the open. "We wuz so scaihed, we
got all tuhned aroun' an' neah went into the fahve-an'-
dime, an' . . . oh, worried!"

Milish and I dined at the same table, and she reminisced
a good deal about her earlier life. She was the only member of our class who had been born blind, and she read
Braille fluently, but there were some surprising gaps in
her knowledge of the world in which she lived. Until
the moment of her introduction to Peg, she had never felt
more of a dog than its back—"jus' a roun' thaing covahed
with haih," she gigglingly admitted. That night in the
Recreation Room, she allowed me to guide her hands over
the rest of Peg's anatomy, and I vividly recall her reluctant fascination with the formation of the paws. From
early childhood until the previous year she had been sent
to a state school for the blind, but was at present living
with her family. Although she was working, as I remember it, in a canning factory, she entertained aspirations as
a professional singer. She had been self-taught to play the
piano, on which she showed surprising versatility with
only three chords and, when coaxed, would sing to us
occasionally, to the delight of Mr. Ballard. At Princeton,
I would have dismissed any of the hillbilly or western

ditties of which her repertory almost entirely consisted as
sheer "corn," but at the Seeing Eye I recognized a sweetness and purity in her voice, particularly in the sugar-
coated strains of "Rose of the Alamo," which defied even
my undergraduate cynicism.

Our most memorable conversation took place in the
station wagon on an unseasonably warm day. We had just
completed a particularly long and brisk walk, and I was
perspiring freely, as I clambered into the back seat and
adjusted my legs around Minnie's furry bulk.

"Gee, Milish, I could sure use a long cold beer right
now."

"Why, Bookaidge!" she said reproachfully. "A nahss
boy lahk yew?"

"What's the matter? Don't you like beer?"

"Too souah! . . . Mah gran'pappy lahks it, though."
She made a noise of disgust and picked up again after a
moment's reflection. "He's got a grea'-big-ole-beahd, an'
when I were little, my motheh used t'make me kiss him,
an' his face were all prickles lahk a haidge-hawg, an' he
smelled of beeah awful. . . . Worried!" She braked, skid-
ding slightly, and when she began again, there was a
smirk in her voice. "Sometimes, he used t'get drunk an'
cahy on wuhss'n a hown dawg with a treed possum."

"What did he do?"

She giggled. "He'd take off his hat an' his shews an' go
down to the hahway, an' shoot!"

"My God!" I gasped. "Who did he shoot at?" I had visions of the feuding mountaineers in the *Esquire* cartoons.

"Oh, he didden have no aim," she reassured me. "He jus' shaht. Bad off!"

Whatever the idiosyncrasies of Milish's early training, I had to admire both her determination and her native intelligence. She grasped the essentials of guide-dog techniques quickly and performed her assigned tasks with cheerful competence. It was difficult on many counts to consider her as "bad off" and impossible to think of her as "worried."

*   *   *

My walks with Mr. Bauermann, although less frequent than those with Militia, were made memorable by the speed with which they took place. Minnie and Duchess were the biggest, fastest, and hardest-pulling dogs in the class, and either hated to be behind the other. As I have already mentioned, this combination of circumstances gave us both a merciless jolting whenever we were paired in "the mastodon marathon" as Mr. Northrup used to call it, but Mr. Bauermann's weight gave him the worst of it. He looked forward eagerly to Sundays, when our only walking was to the Park and back, and spent the greater portion of his time stretched flat on his broad back on his bed, luxuriating in the joys of shoelessness. In place of an afternoon feeding, we presented our dogs with huge beef knuckles.

They were the size of a duck-pin bowling ball, and for more than an hour the sound of these eight bones being rolled about on the bare linoleum floor was like the thunder of celestial bowlers in the old Dutch legend. Soothed by this gentle rumble, Mr. Bauermann was dozing blissfully on his bed one Sunday, when Mr. Northrup called to us to remove the bones from the dogs and harness up for supper. The bedsprings whined in protest as he swung his stockinged feet to the floor close to where Duchess still crunched contentedly. Man's best friend emitted a menacing growl.

"Now, Duchess!" placated Mr. Bauermann. There followed his nervous, but still infectious fat man's laugh. Another growl, clearly audible in the hall where the rest of us were assembling for the trip downstairs, indicated that Mr. Bauermann was making a further attempt to separate Duchess from her bone.

"Now, Duchess! Quit it!" her master commanded sternly, but, an instant later, his voice rumbled into slow laughter again.

"Ye'd best put yer shoes on, Bauermann!" Mr. McNeill called just before descending the stairs. "Don't know as I'd care for 'em meself, but Duchess might just take a fancy to them toes o'yours."

The last member of the class had left the upper floor before Mr. Bauermann had entered the hall, and it was two or three minutes after we had sat down to supper that he came into the dining room. Derisive laughter greeted him from all sides, when Mr. Northrup informed us that Duchess, leashed and harnessed and guiding her master with sedate correctness, was, nevertheless, still triumphantly in possession of her monstrous prize. On the succeeding Sundays, the class pooled its talents in suggesting to Mr. Bauermann various Rube Goldberg devices which might be useful as bone relievers.

* * *

With Mr. Curtiss, my second roommate, a piano tuner from Washington, D.C., the roll call of the little class is complete. A neat, pleasant fellow, a few years older than myself, he made the least impression on me, because his background and temperament were the least unlike my own. I was struck by his facility on the Recreation Room piano, because I had just begun music lessons myself and was haltingly trying to master a stolid arrangement of "Drink to Me Only with Thine Eyes," but I remember him chiefly for a musical anecdote he told me. It was, in itself, only mildly amusing, but I remember it clearly, not for itself, but because it led to a sudden revelation of something which had been going on between me and my classmates.

As I recollect, it concerned the older and younger Johann Strauss. The father made no secret of his contempt for the new harmonies in which his son composed, and, in order to taunt his conservatism, young Johann, returning home late and somewhat in his cups, used to wake the elder Strauss by banging out a few of his despised waltzes upon the piano. When he was certain that the old man had been thoroughly aroused, he would strike a diminished seventh chord upon the keys and take himself off to bed with the lingering dissonance still unresolved. Try as he would to return to his slumbers, the irritable father could only toss and turn until, finally, yielding to the inevitable, he rose from his bed, descended the stairs, and struck the harmonic resolution of the repugnant chord. This suggested a new field for even my limited talents. On the night Mr. Curtiss told me the story, having waited until everyone was in bed, I got up and went in to the Recreation Room piano, where I managed a pretty respectable chord sequence ending on a haunting diminished seventh. Then I returned to my bed without saying a word and waited. Mr. Curtiss said nothing either. Finally, I could bear it no longer.

"God! Doesn't that get you?" I asked.

"Doesn't bother me," Mr. Curtiss remarked sardonically. "You forget. I'm a piano tuner. I'm used to hearing all kinds of horrible sounds."

"I give up," I said, throwing back the covers and getting out of the bed. We were all three giggling like schoolgirls by the time I had returned from the piano, having struck the proper resolution.

Still smiling, as I lay quietly in my bed, I tried to sound the secret of our laughter. There was nothing so terribly funny in the incident. Not in the chord on the Recreation Room piano. Not in Duchess's bone. Not in the verbal battles between Mr. Torbak and Mr. McNeill. Not in the thousand trivialities at which we laughed. And that was another thing. We laughed. Not I laughed, and they laughed, but we laughed. The whole thing reminded me of the Princeton Triangle Club the week before the show opened, when we all got so tired in the almost continuous rehearsals that we laughed at everything. We were stimulated by the fatigue of the common effort, and the nervous energy generated in work sought release in laughter. That was what had happened at the Seeing Eye, I thought, and even more important, what had happened to me was that I had been melted into that laughter. It was the link that joined us all together. It had crept up on me slowly, and it was a surprise to discover it. It was not the first and not the last surprise I found at the Seeing Eye.

The Canine Mathematics

Given: the most intelligent of all the domesticated animals, a complex of instincts and impulses, likes and dislikes, capabilities and limitations.

To Prove: that this animal can be molded into the most nearly perfect instrument for conducting a blind man where he wishes to go with safety and convenience.

Solution: the conditioning methods evolved by the staff of the Seeing Eye on the basis of experience, logic, and the human will.

THUS, LIKE THE FORMULA OF A HIGH-SCHOOL GEOMETRY proposition, I defined my problem at the Seeing Eye, and into this rigorously consistent pattern I sought to fit together the various data which I accumulated as the course progressed. To be sure, there were many missing pieces in the puzzle, but I felt confident that, as I acquired additional bits of information, each would find its place in this scheme of things. The union of dog and master could be achieved only through a complicated equation, but even the seemingly imponderable and unmathematical element of their mutual affection was to be obtained by scientific logic, and, as the practical difficulties of applying these concepts grew more apparent, I became all the more fascinated and determined to unravel the knots under the white light of reason.

According to my mechanistic interpretation, Minnie's various characteristics were first to be graded and then either encouraged or repressed, depending upon whether they facilitated or hindered her work as a guide. The instinct for self-preservation was good, both because it prompted her to avoid dangerous traffic, and because it might be used as the means of attaching dog to master. Hence, Minnie was to receive her life-giving food only from me, and, at mealtimes, I went into the hall, where Mr. Northrup had prepared her feed pan, and returned with it to Minnie, handing it to her personally. Her instinct for self-reproduction would have been an inconvenience, and it had, therefore, been eliminated by a surgical operation. Her atavistic desire to be always in the lead when walking with another dog in the street, a throwback, I supposed, to the primitive epoch when the first wolf in the pack got the largest portion of caribou meat, was undesirable. In order to check it, Mr. Northrup showed me how to suddenly release my hold on the harness handle, so that, stumbling with the forward momentum, she would slow her pace to regain her balance.

The mysterious affinity of dog for master, the product, I conjectured, of centuries of domestication, was to be encouraged in every way, and I never allowed Minnie to be separated from me for an instant, even taking her into the lavatory when I shaved or took a shower. In order to avoid offense to her sensitive nostrils, I did not smoke until she had time to accustom herself to the odor of tobacco. These were but a few among a thousand examples of the way in which I sought to erect from the daily instructions of Mr. Northrup and Mr. Humphrey a sort of positivistic rationale of canine mathematics. It had a strong intellectual appeal, and, in my satisfaction with it, it was a long time before I discovered the missing factor in my increasingly complicated equation.

* * *

The patient thoroughness of the Seeing Eye's teaching methods was no less appealing than the logic of the lessons it taught. Both were amply demonstrated, even before we had been assigned our dogs, and I well remember the morning Mr. Northrup collected us all in the Recreation Room after breakfast.

"Before I take you into Morristown," he began, "I'd like to show you what we call obedience exercises. Mr. Bauermann, you've had a dog before. Would you like to explain to the class what obedience exercises are?"

Mr. Bauermann shifted in his chair, but he made no reply.

"Do you know what they are, Mr. Bauermann?"

"I guess I don't remember." Mr. Bauermann laughed uneasily.

"You're supposed to have done them with your dog every day." There was a brief pause, pregnant with reproof. "Will you tell the class, Mr. McNeill?"

"Why, obedience is when ye make yer dog sit, lie down, rest, fetch, and so on. . . ." Mr. McNeill's dry Scottish accents trailed off on a note of interrogation.

"That's right," Mr. Northrup encouraged, "and we'll go into the details in a moment, but can you tell me why we perform obedience?"

Mr. McNeill coughed slightly. "Why, to check her up, so to speak."

"That's right," Mr. Northrup approved again. "You're all going to make mistakes," he told the class in general. "At one time or another, you'll use the improper command, or try to correct your dog for a mistake she did not make. On the other hand, you will sometimes fail to correct real errors, and you must never attempt to give a correction when your dog is between curbs. Anybody know why not?"

"Dog's gotta have confidence when she's out in the street!" Mr. Bauermann boomed in atonement.

"That's right. Incidentally, for the benefit of the new students," he added, anticipating the question which had already arisen in my mind, "we'll take up corrections later, so don't worry about them for the present. Did you raise your hand, Mr. McNeill?"

"I was just going to tell a little story to illustrate Bauermann's point," he answered, a trifle sententiously, I thought. I was sure Mr. Northrup would put a stop to this interruption, but Mr. McNeill's even tenor droned on.

"Crossin' the street on m'way to work one mornin'," he began, as if launching into a bedtime story, "a chap of my acquaintance sings out: 'Hey, McNeill, where're ye goin'?' Till we gets to the other side o' the street, I says nothin'." Having uttered these words with calm deliberation, Mr. McNeill paused for a moment to let their full import take effect.

"When we're up on the curb," he continued, "I turn Gyp about, and we marches back. The fella says, 'What's the matter, McNeill? Didn't ye hear me the first time?'

" 'I'm not deaf,' I says. 'I heared ye, all right, but I never interrupt Gyp when she's out in the center of the road.' " With the measured righteousness of the pedagogue, Mr. McNeill concluded his tale on a note of subdued triumph.

"That was the right thing to do," soothed Mr. Northrup, without a trace of the impatience I had expected, but he hurried on quickly. "Well, class, because of the mistakes you will make yourself, and because of your occasional failures to correct your dog's mistakes, you may lose your authority over her a little. To keep her up to the mark, we perform obedience exercises—every day, Mr. Bauermann— with the dog on long leash. When she's on the leash, you can tell whether she's obeying your commands, and you can reward or correct her accordingly. That way, she'll get to know that you know what you're doing and that you mean what you say. Is that clear?"

I was pleased with the logic of this approach to dog education, and, as Mr. Northrup proceeded, I was satisfied that the Seeing Eye had not confined its efforts to the education of dogs alone.

"Upon the command 'Juno, come!' your dog approaches you from in front, circles around your right side and behind you, and comes to a stop at your left, because that is the position in which you always use her."

When Mr. Northrup had completed his explanations, he rehearsed us all individually, again assuming the role of the overworked Juno. The verbal command to come was to be accompanied by an encouraging jerk of the leash held in the right hand, but Mrs. Clay tugged at it so violently as to snatch it quite out of his grasp and send it flying across the room. On a second trial, she was gentler, and Juno plodded across the floor, circled, and was just getting down on all fours at her left, when Mrs. Clay shattered the dramatic illusion.

"My skirt!" she said nervously. "My skirt's caught."

"It's all right, Mrs. Clay," Mr. Northrup pacified. "You must remember that you start off with the leash in your right hand, so when I go around you, you must pass it to your left hand, or it will wind around your legs. Now, let's try it again."

They did try it again, but hardly had Mr. Northrup's footsteps approached her side, when the lady shrieked: "It's happening again, Mr. Northrup. It's happening again!"

"Take it easy, Mrs. Clay," Mr. Northrup laughed. "You must pass the leash *behind* you. When I circle, you transfer the leash from your right hand to your left behind your back, not over your stomach."

"Oh, I see," Mrs. Clay answered with a penitence which suggested that she had previously suspected her masculine Juno of foul play. "Oh, dear, Mr. Northrup. I get so confused. You see, I'm the nervous type."

Her successor, Mr. Torbak, who was not the nervous type, proved to be no less confused. The command, "Juno, sit," was to be accompanied by a slight upward jerk of the leash held in the right hand and downward shove upon

Juno's rump with the left. Mr. Torbak began swimmingly, but, when he came to this part of the performance, perhaps stagestruck by the sudden public notice it brought him, he became oblivious of the distinction between right and left.

"No, Mr. Torbak," Mr. Northrup corrected, kneeling beside him on the floor, "down with your left hand and up with your right."

"Chuno, zitt!" rumbled Mr. Torbak.

"Wait a minute! Down with your left hand, up with your right, and . . ."

"Chuno, ZITT!" he thundered and the heavy thump which immediately followed told me that the would-be Juno had been literally if only temporarily floored.

"Take it easy, Mr. Torbak, please," Mr. Northrup protested as he picked himself up slowly. "Look! Your left hand pushes down on my hindquarters, not my head. This is your left hand. This" (there was a resounding smack) "is my hindquarters, my tail, my butt!"

I fancied I heard Mrs. Clay gasp, but even the vulgar precision of Mr. Northrup's terminology did not immediately clarify his impetuous pupil's confusion, and, before the lesson was over, I had developed a firm confidence in the patience of our human Juno.

* * *

With the substitution of Minnie for Mr. Northrup, I discovered further evidence of the care with which the

Seeing Eye had worked out its problems. Obedience was performed daily before lunch after the second outing in the Park, not in the Park itself, but in the adjacent driveway. The Park was the dogs' playground, a place of "recreation," such as it was, and, with characteristic consideration for the canine point of view, the Seeing Eye had ruled that the stern call of duty should not invade its carefree confines.

Not that any of the dogs seemed to regard the performance of obedience as a particularly onerous task. Indeed, their very delight in it raised another problem. Minnie was so eager for the rewards of praise that, by anticipating and obeying as yet unuttered commands, she came near to defeating the avowed purpose of the exercises. She was particularly fond of fetching, and on several occasions she impatiently snatched the glove I was drawing from my pocket before I had had a chance to throw it, circling behind me quickly, and returning to my left side in wagging triumph. I was instructed to discourage this lack of restraint by sometimes altering the usual sequence of commands, but the fact was that the Seeing Eye did not and could not require of its dogs that robotlike discipline which carries off the blue ribbon in the obedience classes of dog shows. The reasons for this should have been immediately obvious, for their practical application underlay the entire course. But it was some time before I grasped their true significance despite the blunt directness with which Mr. Humphrey had explained them in one of his earliest lectures.

"The one thing you people have got to get clear right at the beginning," he announced, "is that you can't make these dogs do anything." He stressed each syllable, as if he were delivering an ultimatum, and, mentally shifting my balance, I tried to guess at its direction. "Now, I can make dogs do things. If I want to make a hunting dog retrieve, I can take him out into a field with a dead bird, turn him loose, and, if he doesn't go straight for it, if he turns to the right or to the left, I can burn his tail with a B-B gun, until he learns." After a pause, he continued with the same quiet emphasis. "Now, you can't do that, and the reason you can't do that is because you're blind. Your dogs will obey you only because they want to, and they'll want to only so long as you keep rewarding them for what they do."

Mr. Humphrey was not one to linger upon abstract generalities, and, in a sense having said it all, he proceeded to illustrate by example.

"Now, don't for a minute imagine that your dogs don't know you're blind. We had a man here once who thought he could bully his dog. He'd jerk her around on the leash and holler at her, and that poor dog just couldn't do anything right. We warned him, but he wouldn't believe us. I thought I knew what was coming, so I just kept an eye on him and waited. The dog took it for quite a while, but sure enough, one fine day she walked that man smack," and here Mr. Humphrey slapped his palm on the wooden chair arm, "into a lamp post." Thinking of the force with which Minnie pulled me along the street, I winced, and one of the students sitting near me whistled under his breath.

"I could have stopped it," Mr. Humphrey admitted. "It shook him up quite a bit, but it taught him his lesson better than any words of ours could."

I decided that Mr. Humphrey was not a man to be trifled with and riveted my attention even more firmly upon his words.

"Another fellow we had here worked out fine all during the course, and I thought he was set, but when he got home, an unusual trouble developed. His dog didn't bump him into anything, and she was a fine worker in traffic. The only thing was that after a while she seemed to dislike work. They'd start out together all right, and, all of a sudden, she'd bring him right back home. He couldn't figure it out." I was struck by a vivid mental picture of the unfortunate man, rising early each morning, eating a brisk breakfast, and departing for work, humming cheerily, only to find himself, within five minutes, mysteriously returned to his own doorstep, and I laughed. But Mr. Humphrey's tone had become serious again. "He wrote us a letter, and we sent an instructor down there to investigate. This is what we found. The man loved his dog all right, and in the house everything was fine. He'd get down on the floor and roughhouse with her, and they had a great time. But, out on the street, he was taking her for granted. It was 'Juno, forward!' 'Juno, this!' and 'Juno, that!' but never," and here the imperative tone of his voice gave way to a warmth which startled me, " 'Juno, atta *good* girl!' The dog got the idea that the only place her master really liked her was at home, so, whenever she got a chance, she took him there as fast as she could."

It was a warming story with a clearly pointed message and, although something about Mr. Humphrey's personality made me uncomfortable, I began to look forward to the little talks in the Recreation Room.

* * *

The beautiful simplicity of the guiding principle of reward and correction became more complicated in the mechanics of practical application, but, as the system gradually unfolded, I was repeatedly impressed by its logical clarity. Corrections took three main forms, all of which were verbal in essence, because, as Mr. Humphrey pointed out, any physical chastisement which taught the dog to fear her blind master's hands would prove a serious handicap. The mildest form of correction was the phrase, "Hopp, hopp." It was pronounced with a rising inflection to accelerate Juno's speed, dispel her hesitation, or to steady her wavering attention. "Juno, quit it!" spoken with some degree of menace, cautioned against such wayward activities as growling, shortcutting, or failing to respond to a previous command. The severest of all was the terrible imprecation, "Pfui!" So sensitive were our dogs to the shame of this condemnation, intoned with the utmost venom, that we students were not permitted to use it at all during the first weeks of the course. Whenever required, it was administered instead by Mr. Northrup. Our dogs must be firmly convinced of their new masters' benevolent intentions before being exposed to the more villainous side of their natures.

In the most flagrant breaches of etiquette, wetting or dirtying the house, repeated barking or growling, fighting, or stealing, one physical supplement was added to these verbal corrections. This consisted in a sharp jerk upon the leash accompanied by an awful "Pfui," and, done with sufficient strength it could upset the dog's balance and even cause her to lose her footing. It was not to be considered as an end in itself, however, but merely as a means of emphasizing or reinforcing the basic disciplinary instrument, which was, first and always, the master's displeasure as expressed in his tone of voice. Mr. Northrup assured me that a dog's sensitivity to pain was much less than that of a human, but I was soon convinced by experience that their sensitivity to shame was, if anything, far greater. As a result, the administration of these corrections was often a heavy burden of responsibility, fraught with pitfalls which it took me months, even years, to recognize.

"When you're giving your dog a correction," Mr. Humphrey warned us, "there's no need of making a great fuss. Your dogs aren't deaf, and you don't have to shout. It's the tone and not the volume of your voice that counts. All that's needed is 'Juno, pfui!' " He fairly whispered the words, but with such an inflection of malice that Minnie, who had apparently been sound asleep with her chin resting on my instep, started, raised her head quickly, and bent her attention nervously on the speaker.

"Another thing," he continued. "A leash correction doesn't demand that you wave your arms like a windmill. In six or eight inches, you can get all the force you'll need ninety-nine times in a hundred. People don't like to see you abusing your dogs in the street, and they'll think you are if you thrash around and make a big scene. A good leash correction ought to be given so that a person five feet away won't even notice it."

The warning was clear enough, but over a year was to pass before I discovered its full implications. There were times when I found the act of giving a correction surprisingly disturbing to my emotional equilibrium. Hurrying along on a bright spring day, or a wet fall day, or a cold winter day, on the way to a class, or a meal, or a dentist appointment, mentally preoccupied with my private thoughts and feelings, I would suddenly stumble, perhaps, because Minnie had failed to pause at a curb. Instantly, I must banish every other consideration from my mind, externally making a proper show of my displeasure to Minnie while inwardly trying to preserve an objective calm, ready to alter my tone from the most venomous "Pfui" to the most ecstatic "Atta *good* girl!" the instant she had returned to obedience, and all the time thinking that I was late for the dentist appointment. My acting was good enough for Minnie, and, because I never encountered any of those difficulties Mr. Humphrey had described in his anecdotes of other students, I was satisfied that it kept the necessary balance between rewards and corrections. Hot and flushed with the emotional exercise of the correction, I went on my way, unaware that I had overplayed my role before an unseen audience. Ostrichlike, I never realized the possible effect of my appearance upon the seeing public which, in its turn, was totally ignorant of the methods of guide-dog technique and, therefore, of the meaning of my actions.

One recurrent source of difficulty is, perhaps, the simplest illustration of the way a misunderstanding could develop. There were many slightly raised flagstone walks on the Princeton campus, and, as the strain of Minnie's pull upon the harness handle tugged me to the extreme right-hand edge, I often turned my ankle and stumbled. This, of course, required a "Pfui," which I, in my forgetfulness, and really irritated by the repeated infraction on Minnie's part, thundered in Shakespearean fashion. The casual observer, suddenly attracted by the sound of my voice, might see only my angered expression, distorted posture, and upraised foot. It is only conjecture on my part—for, in all the ten years I have been using a guide, I have never been approached by a spectator at the moment of a correction—but I believe that this circumstance was probably responsible for the fiction, reported to the S.P.C.A. four times within a year, that I had kicked Minnie on the street. Ultimately, the matter was brought to the attention of the Seeing Eye authorities, who, in turn, informed me of it. Taken utterly by surprise, I was indignant, humiliated, baffled, and shamed by turns, feeling that I had somehow betrayed a sacred trust. It was a vast relief when Mr. Debetaz, the chief instructor, made a special trip to Princeton to check into my conduct and informed me, after taking us for a test walk, that our good co-ordination could not have been the product of such a relationship as the reports had described. Nevertheless, the experience still haunts me, and it has taught me the fallacy of the mathematical equation of years ago which had failed to include the seeing public as a factor.

Our sheerly physical difficulties were more amusing. One of Minnie's most annoying habits, when walking in the rain, was to seek partial shelter under the awnings of the shop windows which lined the street. In so doing, she often brought my head directly in line with the dripping fringes which, just ticking the crown of my scalp as we paced along, streamed icy rivulets down the back of my neck. In such a contingency I was supposed to stop, pound the offending overhang with my free hand, and mutter a vindictive "Pfui!" In Morristown, barring a speed which often took me past the awning before I could raise my arm and left me pawing the damp atmosphere several feet beyond, this procedure was possible. Later, in Princeton, when only the spur of necessity took me to the shopping district in the rain, my free hand was usually clutching some recent purchase. After a conscientious effort to follow instructions by squeezing a bundle of groceries between trembling knees had cost me a dozen eggs and a jar of mayonnaise, I guiltily ducked my head and feigned unconcern at the slow trickle of rain water between my hunched shoulder blades.

The prescribed method for discouraging the demonstrative Minerva from playfully jumping up on people demanded even greater physical co-ordination. The corrective formula was eminently logical. It recommended grasping the forepaws and stepping "gently, but firmly" on her hind feet. To begin with, the first sign of Minnie's over-exuberance was generally a well-aimed paw to my unsuspecting solar plexus. Next, I had to grope about in the darkness to locate the dancing forepaws. Finally, once grasped and raised, I had to face the prospect of a grotesque rumba with a feminine partner whose ecstatic delight was alternately licking and biting my hands. Even if all desire to play the part of a disciplinarian had not long since left me by this time, it would have been impossible to step upon her hind paws without mashing them, and I soon decided that this part of Seeing Eye mathematics was suitable only for professional ballet dancers.

* * *

The system of rewards was just as logical and far simpler than that of corrections, but it took some time for its full implications to become rooted in my mind. There were dozens of ways to win Minnie's affection as a pet. Personal care and feeding, periods of play, gentle treatment, the avoidance of offense to her sensitivity to unpleasant odors and sudden loud noises, and above all, constant association (which, I confess, made her seem at times like a fifty-nine pound ball and chain) all made her a loyal companion. In harness, however, the uncompromising demands of duty, aside from an occasional pat, could be compensated only through the praise I bestowed with my voice, a fact which I could not afford to forget for a moment. Even in the simple obedience exercises, in which I required her to come, sit and lie down three times alternately, sit at rest, and fetch, the sirupy inflections of "Minnie, atta *good* girl!" were demanded a minimum of thirteen times, and the three-minute trip to the Park cost me over thirty installments of this verbal payment. At the end of a week, I fancied I could hear myself mumbling the words in my sleep, and yet it was imperative that each of these endless repetitions should sound as rapturous as the last. All this was clearly intelligible to my rational consciousness, but practical experience continued to unfold further revelations.

I remember having trouble with Minnie one evening on my way down to dinner. She had a tendency to stop too far from the edge of curbs and stairs for me to feel their outlines with my extended right foot, and on this occasion I could not inveigle her to approach for the descent of the final flight of steps. Absurdly marooned on the second landing, I was near desperation when, in the midst of my assorted "Hopp, hopps" and "Quit its," Mr. Northrup's voice came up to us from below.

"What's a matter, Minnie?" he cooed sympathetically.

As if by magic, the recalcitrant Minnie moved forward to the edge of the stair, and we descended smoothly. Mr. Northrup waited for us at the foot and followed us into the dining room in silence. When I had taken my seat, he joined us at the little table.

"Did I hear you stamp your pretty little foot on the stair just now?" he jeered in a low voice.

I blushed involuntarily at the words, but I had an explanation. "She wouldn't go to the edge of the stair," I argued, "and I was stamping my foot to draw her attention to it."

"Oh," his tone relaxed. "Well, you shouldn't have done that. She's been taught to react away from sounds like that. You see, the way we correct a dog who goes up or down steps or curbs too quickly, so that you stumble, is to put her at sit in front of them and stamp on them. That's why she wouldn't go forward. She was really doing the right thing under the circumstances."

"I see," I said, wondering with a tinge of despair whether I would ever master the thousand and one details of the course.

"You want to watch your tone of voice," he added soberly. "You had Minnie all worried up there. The minute I spoke to her, she started to wag her tail."

That was all there was to the incident, but it brought home to me forcibly, for the first time, that it was important, even while working, that Minnie should wag her tail.

* * *

If I could forget the proper vocal inflection in so simple a task as the descent to the dining room, my problems multiplied tenfold in the far more difficult conditions I encountered on the streets of Morristown. As Minnie tugged me along, I was engrossed in the sheerly physical problem of my response to the warning signals which came up to me from the harness handle. There were abrupt stops at curbs, changes of pace or lateral movements to avoid oncoming pedestrians, and little hesitations to indicate rough places in the sidewalk.

My confidence was further shaken by periodic lapses of memory as to my exact itinerary. Pounding along the pavement, my relief at having successfully maneuvered an intricate crossing would disappear in a sudden thrill of panic like that of a lost child in a strange city. I crossed a gravel driveway which I could not recall from a previous trip, and it set me to wondering. Should I have crossed and turned right at the last intersection, instead of turning right and crossing? Expectantly, I waited for some familiar landmark to restore my orientation. At the next crossing there should be a service station, identifiable by the hum of gas pumps whose bells chimed warningly at each gallon injection. Or was that the following block? Minnie's pace did not slacken, but the distance to the next curb seemed suddenly to double, and, making rapid mental calculations as to the route thus far, I tried to conceal my embarrassing predicament from the unseen glances of passing pedestrians, Mr. Northrup, or—perish the thought!—the Argus-eyed Mr. Humphrey himself.

My anxiety imparted itself, somehow, to Minnie, and when we had finally reached the curb, sensing the impatience with which I waited for my walking partner to come up, she attempted to dart off to the left without waiting for a command. This necessitated a correction, during which I must maintain my self-possession in order to control the modulations of my voice. In a cold sweat of concentration I waited, as expressionless as an Egyptian statue and inwardly yearning for the cigarette I would smoke in the station wagon.

I was to have the like experience dozens of times in the first months after leaving Morristown. On my very first solo voyage in the relatively unfamiliar country around our new home in Litchfield, Minnie and I were lost for almost three hours. Having failed in every practical application of my mathematical formula, I ultimately resigned myself to the hope that Minnie's ravenous appetite, whetted by an eight-mile walk over snowy roads, would direct her, and her chastened master behind her, to the food pan in the kitchen. It did, but I still have not the faintest notion what unblazed trails we pioneered that day.

A month later, emboldened by my new success at Princeton, I invited a girl for the weekend, and, having escorted her to her lodging at midnight, I set off blithely for my room on the other side of the campus. The route was a simple one, but, at the lower end of University Place, in a terrain which I knew like the palm of my hand, I became suddenly, inexplicably, and quite hopelessly lost. I crossed and recrossed the wide expanse of street which I knew to be adjacent to McCarter Theater, but I could make no landfall. There was no one of whom to inquire the way, and the occasional cars which sped by over the deserted streets only further confused my orientation by proceeding undamaged through what, only a moment before, I had imagined to be the sites of solid stone structures. As in Litchfield, I finally determined to abandon Seeing Eye mathematics, and, putting Minnie at sit and rest on the sidewalk, set out to explore for myself. A dozen steps away, I hurtled four feet to the steel and cinder track from the railroad station platform. In a flash, Minnie had jumped down beside me in a panic of nervous devotion. She licked my face excitedly as I sprawled across the ties, bruised but unhurt, and relieved at last to know where I was.

"I wonder, now, Miss Minerv," I laughed, "did ye bring your racquet with ye?" And slowly, I limped to my feet.

*   *   *

Little by little, as the course progressed, the rigid outlines of the logical edifice I had been attempting to build began to obscure, and this was no less true of my successes than of my failures. The more closely I lived with my experience, the more mysterious seemed to me Minnie's conscientious enthusiasm for her work. I became dimly aware that I could not explain it upon the strictly rational premises with which I had begun. Yet experience confirmed its existence every time she eagerly wiggled into the outstretched harness and then waited impatiently for me to buckle it under her gently heaving chest. Neither could mathematics provide an infallible guide as to my conduct when following her through the maze of traffic and pedestrians, the curbs and steps, the trees and lamp posts, the baby carriages and express wagons which dotted the walks of Morristown. How was I to know, when Minnie lurched suddenly to the left, whether she was preparing to chase a squirrel or pulling me around an open manhole? The idea that this depended upon mere guesswork irritated me, and I recoiled from it toward the contemplation of the academic certainties I had been able to establish, but the problem persisted. Time and again,

Mr. Northrup broke his self-imposed silence. "Follow your dog, Mr. Putnam," he would shout. "She's trying to take you around an orange crate. Follow your dog!"

We had been at the Seeing Eye about ten days, and I was still stubbornly wrestling with this problem when, at dinner one night, Mr. Northrup announced that Mr. Humphrey would give a short lecture in the Recreation Room at eight o'clock. With that sixth sense for the unusual which one acquires under an institutional regime, I felt, somehow, that this was to be an extraordinary session, and, as we assembled to wait for the speaker, I lighted a cigarette uneasily. I had had a poor trip that afternoon, and my depression grew deeper as I lay back in the comfortable chair. When Mr. Humphrey strode in, his curt greeting made it obvious that he was prepared to lose no time coming to the point, and I straightened up attentively.

"The main thing you people have got to learn," he articulated impressively, "is to trust the signals your dog gives you. You'll be just as unpopular with your dog, if you try to lead her, as a girl who tries to lead her dancing partner." The simile struck me as being peculiarly inept. I could not conceive of any woman so daring as to usurp Mr. Humphrey's masculine prerogative in the ballroom. But, following his usual line, the speaker was proceeding from the general to the particular, drawing upon his infallible weapon—past experience—and it would not do to allow my thoughts to meander.

"We had a man here a few years back who always took a step after his dog had stopped. We tried to tell him, but he simply refused to believe us. He was one of these people who always knew better."

Mr. Humphrey seemed to glare for a moment, and I shifted uncomfortably, wondering whether there was any significance in the fact that he had said "these people," rather than "those people."

"We didn't mind his stumbling a bit at curbs, but, out in traffic, it was really dangerous. I was afraid something would happen to him, so, finally, I decided to take matters into my own hands." He cleared his throat and continued. "The next day, I got out my car and waited for him at an intersection. Pretty soon, he came along and started across. I headed the car for the two of them, and, sure enough, the dog stopped, but the man stepped out in front of her. So—" Mr. Humphrey seemed to shrug at the inexorable exigencies of his fate—"I just picked him up on the bumper, nice and easy, and carried him a few feet. It didn't hurt him, but, when I helped him up and showed him the dog, still standing beside the car, he simply *had* to believe me. After that, we never had any more trouble with him."

Whatever its educational value, I felt a sort of threat in this grim parable.

"Now, what I want to point out," he went on, "is that we can correct your mechanical mistakes, if you pay attention, and we can teach you a lot, but it's up to you to be-lieve what your dog tells you. You've got to have the courage of your dog's convictions. We were able to give that man a dog, but he had to learn confidence the hard way."

Mr. Humphrey spoke for some time, but my thoughts continually reverted to his opening anecdote. For whom had it been intended? For me? But, I argued, Mrs. Clay was a worse offender than I in this particular. I was still pondering its true significance at the close of the lecture, but, as I was returning to my room to harness Minnie for the last trip to the Park, Mr. Torbak interrupted my thoughts.

"Dot Homphree!" he muttered in a delighted *sotto voce*. "He summting, my Got!" He was immensely pleased. "Lest dime I'm here, I'm valking alunk, gat lust . . . didden know vare I vuss. . . . My Got! Alluva sodden, I stick my foot in de lake!" His voice rose to a hoarse shout. "Vuss my shoe *vat*!" he roared, doubling up with laughter.

The picture of Mr. Torbak's brimming shoe dispelled my gloomy forebodings, and I laughed, too.

Mr. Torbak's voice became confidential again. "Dot Homphree! He comes alunk, graps my shulder, toins me roundt, gifs me poosh." Mr. Torbak's bronchial rumble soared forth again. " 'Vare de hal you tink you goink!'

he sass. 'My Got! You go dat vay!' Gifs me pig poosh. He summting."

And Mr. Torbak stumped off down the hall, still ruminating delightedly on the comic genius of "dot Homphree."

As my amusement ebbed, I was suddenly seized with the strange irrational conviction that Mr. Torbak's story had an important bearing upon my own dilemma. In the silence of the Park, I followed Minnie around in a speculative trance. I seemed to have developed a personal antipathy for Mr. Humphrey. Was I afraid he would pick me up on the bumper of his car? Absurd! There was something else. And to say he did not talk the same language was a meaningless platitude. Neither did any of the others; yet I felt a warm affection for all of them. It was that we did not seem to be talking or, rather, thinking about the same thing. That was it! It came in a flash. Mr. Humphrey had been trying to impress upon me how a blind man could adjust himself to a guide dog. I had been thinking in terms of how a dog could be molded into a guide for a blind man, but I had not truly identified myself with that blind man. I had been trying to think as an instructor, making the whole thing into a sort of intellectual game, mathematical, rigid, and absolute. I wanted rational explanations for everything. My intellectual vanity would have been infuriated if Mr. Humphrey had given me a "pig poosh," but Torbak, innocent of academic nonsense, had accepted its rough guidance, unquestioningly and with good humor. I almost laughed aloud there in the darkness of the Park. My blindness, the very first thing upon which Mr. Humphrey had laid his emphasis, must be a perpetual unknown in the guide-dog equation, and, having fully recognized this fact for the first time, I began to see.

CHAPTER V

The Daily Fugue

A DAY AT THE SEEING EYE HAD A CURIOUSLY POLYPHONIC quality. Different levels of emotional experience ran along side by side like the voices of a fugue, now one and now another predominating, so that it was often difficult to distinguish the parts from the whole. Passages of intensive physical and nervous concentration were suddenly interrupted, at the other end of the scale, by flights of spontaneous amusement in the society of my fellow students. The purely intellectual strains of my interest in the process of guide-dog education were played against the warmer tones of my growing affection for Minnie, considered merely as a companion, while the more somber treatment accorded her as a delicate and efficient piece of machinery underscored the social and moral motives of the institution which had produced her. And like a running ground bass beneath them all were my entirely subjective ambitions for success and fears of failure.

Contradictory as were these moods—the subjective goads of the will alternating with the objective interests of the intellect, the spasms of physical exertion and the bursts of relaxing laughter, the consciousness of personal isolation and the sense of communal *esprit*, the waves of an almost paternal devotion for Minnie and a sort of filial response to the ethical demands of the Seeing Eye—they were so closely integrated into the incidents of the daily routine that to consider them apart from it is nearly impossible. In reality, this routine varied in many particulars as the course progressed, but viewed from the vantage point of my study chair on a rainy morning nearly ten years later, it appears so unchanging that the occurrences of several weeks fall easily into the pattern of a single day.

This day usually began for me with the sound of voices floating fitfully through my consciousness. One of my roommates had left the door open on his way to the lavatory, and from the corridor there echoed the sounds of Mr. Torbak's low rumble, Mr. McNeill's cheerful tenor, and an occasional laugh from the good-natured Mr. Bauermann. They were always up earlier than Mr. Ballard, Mr. Curtiss, and myself, a younger and sleepier trio, and their unfailing morning heartiness always seemed a rebuke to my laconic torpor. The gradual quickening of my senses reminded me of stiffened muscles and a frame a trifle cramped in the iron bed, and I rolled over for a last moment of relaxation, but the squeak of the bed springs betrayed me. Minnie, alert for any signs of life from her prostrate master, started quickly to her feet and began to lick my face noisily.

"Take it easy, Minerv," I protested feebly, trying simultaneously to pat her and push her away.

"Atta *good* girl, Minnie," soothed Mr. Curtiss from across the room. "If your lazy master won't get up and wash his face, you just do it for him."

I creaked to a sitting position and swung my feet over the opposite side of the bed from where Minnie was administering her unwelcome ablutions. This offered me but a scant respite, however, for, whenever I changed my position in the room, the enthusiastic Minerv dived under the bed, bumped along noisily on her elbows, and emerged triumphant on the side nearest me. Now, I had to move quickly to avoid a playful nip on the ankle. She had another disturbing habit, I had discovered, which my future roommates at Princeton were also to learn to their cost. With tail waving amiably, she would approach her unwary and unshod victim and then suddenly, as if with malicious intent, placing one of her feet on top of his, indulge in a long, satisfying stretch which dug her claws cruelly into the tender flesh of his instep. Many a morning have my ears been smitten with shrieks of pain from both my own and other throats at her treachery. In a word, the only sound defense, once awakened by Minnie, was to rise and dress as quickly as possible. At the Seeing Eye, I generally had the additional incentive of being well behind schedule.

By the time I had washed and brushed my teeth in the lavatory across the hall, most of my fellow students had already finished dressing. My recourse was to pull on a coat and pants over my pajamas, slip my feet into socks and moccasins, and add an overcoat which, with a carefully adjusted muffler, effectively concealed my inner undress. During this process, I could hear the conversation of my classmates in the corridor, as they assembled at the top of the stairs for the trip to the Park.

"Hey, Tobaccy," Mr. McNeill quipped. "Ye've got Pilot's harness wrong side fore. What're ye plannin' to do? Back him downstairs?"

Mrs. Clay giggled, but Mr. Torbak only grunted.

"Ah b'lieve Mr. McNeill's th' only Scotchman evah kissed the Blarney stone," Miss Burke said. "Ain't that right, Mr. Torbak?"

"Scotsman, not Scotchman," Mr. McNeill corrected.

" 'Scoose me!" Militia apologized elaborately. "Bad off!"

"Tobaccy don't want his dog to see where he's goin'," Mr. McNeill resumed, "just where he's been."

As I came into the hall, his banter was interrupted by the simultaneous arrival of Mr. Northrup, and we began the descent to the Park.

* * *

Like everything else at the Seeing Eye, the trip to the Park was ruled by a prescribed etiquette, designed to afford the maximum in the education of both dogs and students. We proceeded single file at intervals sufficient to guarantee ample clearance, and each student closed the front door behind him, in order to give his successor practice in finding the handle independently. At each of the several turns, curbs, and driveways, we stopped and waited until our immediate predecessor had negotiated the next phase of the route. One driveway, in particular, proved an unfortunate bottleneck in the early days of the course. For reasons which we could not explain (but which were probably related to the trouble I had had with Minnie on the stair landing), Mrs. Clay's Vera seemed determined not to budge, once arrived at this singularly unprepossessing locale. As the members of the class who were unfortunate enough to have gotten behind her shivered in the cold dawn, Mrs. Clay braced herself for the silent struggle.

"Vera, forward!" she would command. Being from Missouri, Mrs. Clay pronounced the word as if it were spelled "farward," but forward or farward, Vera, too, it seemed, was from Missouri and maintained a statuesque immobility.

"Vera, farward," Mrs. Clay repeated encouragingly. The other dogs were manifestly impatient to get to the Park after the long night indoors, but Vera was seemingly entranced.

"Vera Clay!" her mistress scolded, in her exasperation entirely overlooking the prescribed formula for command. "You go farward this very instant!"

Mr. Ballard used to be very nearly beside himself in his eagerness to give advice, but, from the moment of his encounter with Mr. Torbak, he refrained from offering any suggestions. In time, however, Vera's strange psychological block disappeared, and Mrs. Clay, to whom these daily battles had become a nightmare, never failed to remark, with a kind of wondering disbelief, after a smooth trip to the Park: "You know, it's getting so I almost like to come down here."

Once in the Park, we removed the dogs' harnesses and followed them around on long leash, as they sniffed out the particular piece of gravel most appealing for their purposes. The morning air was sharp and cold. As we were approaching the shortest day of the year, it must still have been quite dark, and every sound carried with the clear quiet ring of night. Periodically, Mr. Northrup's voice echoed hollowly over the yard.

"Back this way, Mr. Torbak. You're too close to the

other class." Since the dogs of the two classes were unknown to each other, we were never allowed to mingle and
were strictly bounded to one half of the rectangle.

"Keep Minnie away from Martha, Mr. Putnam. She's
trying to do number two." As I pulled the playful Minnie
away, Mr. Northrup's footsteps crunched over the gravel
toward Martha, pausing at a little distance from her, and
then advancing again, as he scooped up her stool in a
shovel to deposit it in a galvanized iron can on one side of
the Park.

"Miss Burke," the ghostly voice called again. "Peg likes
the north end. Take her up there. I shouldn't have to tell
you these things by this time."

"Worried!" commented the irrepressible Militia, march-
ing off briskly. "Come on, Paig."

There was something absurd in the seriousness with
which we came to regard the daily routine of canine
catharsis, but I could not ignore the fact that the second
timers, more experienced than the novices in its mysteries,
were always finished before us. Mr. Torbak's morning
shout of "Bilutt, detsh a goodt poy!" would long since have
died upon the silent air, as Mrs. Clay, Miss Burke, and I
still lingered in the chill dawn.

*　　*　　*

Back in the warm house I had ample time to re-dress at
my leisure. As I moved from my bureau to the closet and
from the closet to the chair, Minnie bumped back and

forth underneath the bed, apparently enthralled by the progress of my toilet. When it was complete, I put her back in her harness and joined the others at the top of the stairs for the dining-room convoy. We sat at little tables along the left wall of the room, while the other class sat on the right. In contradiction to Emily Post, Seeing Eye etiquette dictated that we sit down as soon as we had reached our seats, in order to get our dogs out of the way. Minnie curled up peacefully at my feet, and to ensure that she stayed there, I placed one foot over the end of the leash next to her collar, lopping the other end over my knee.

Breakfast began pleasantly. I was thoroughly awake after the outing in the Park, and my tablemates, Mr. Curtiss and Militia Dixie, were lively conversationalists. Halfway through the first cup of coffee, however, I became aware of a growing sense of uneasiness about the impending trip into Morristown. Even after my inner "reconciliation" with Mr. Humphrey, this mental malaise always increased when he was present. Although he ate breakfast in his own home, he frequently arrived at the Seeing Eye before the classes were ready to begin their morning round of work. He rarely sat down for a second cup of coffee, preferring, instead, to pace restlessly up and down the dining room, his rubber soles squeaking on the linoleum floor. He had the air of a top sergeant overlook-

ing a platoon of raw recruits and talking to his corporals,
the instructors, about the plans for that day's training. His
energy seemed to drain away all of mine, and I waited only
until Mr. Northrup had given the orders of the day to
leave the table and return upstairs. It was a relief to discover that, as usual, I had been assigned to the first shift.

Outside on the front porch, waiting with my com-
panions for Mr. Northrup to bring the station wagon
around, my anxiety became more oppressive. I felt like a
small boy waiting for the school bus on examination day,
and, like him, I tried to ease my nervous tension by going
over in my mind the lessons of the previous week. The
illusion was heightened, later in the course, when we
abandoned the use of the station wagon in favor of a real
bus, which stopped just across the road from the school
grounds. State law demanded that the dogs wear muzzles
for these trips, and Minnie was miserable in hers, licking
and snuffling at it with ears drooping abjectly. This had its
compensations, for in soothing her uneasiness I became
superior to my own. Nevertheless, the trip was an ordeal
for both of us, and we were mutually relieved when it was
over and I had replaced the clammy muzzle in my overcoat pocket.

On sunny days, we generally preferred to wait our turns
with Mr. Northrup sitting on the bench just outside the
little bus depot. Minnie sat erect with twitching ears,

alert for every sound and movement among the hurrying pedestrians and busy traffic in the square behind us. She was entirely preoccupied with the immediate present, but my thoughts were engaged in reviewing the order of the route we would traverse that day and repeating over and over to myself the injunctions of the past. I remember in particular one fine fall morning before our first trial of "the high-school route." It was longer and more difficult than anything we had yet tried, and, although we were not expected to have memorized it perfectly the first time, I thought I had gotten Mr. Northrup's description pretty well by heart. Militia Dixie and Mr. McNeill were already off on the first expedition, and Mr. Bauermann sat with Duchess a little to my left.

"Cigarette?" he asked.

"Thanks, I've got one," I said.

"Well, if you've got more than one, I'd appreciate your giving it to me." We both laughed.

"Oh, I'm sorry," I said, taking out my pack. "I guess I was thinking too hard about the route."

"I think I remember it all right. All you've got to do is get Mr. Northrup to let Duchess lead the whole way, and we'll both be happy. Boy! She almost pulls my arm out of the socket every time Minnie gets in front of her."

"Let me see if I've got it straight." I said, "We start on our left, and the first curb we come to is Water Street. It comes in on a slight diagonal, and the other side has a high curb and a deep gutter. I remember because I got wet up to the ankle in it the other day."

"That's one way of learning," Mr. Bauermann said. "You're right so far."

"O.K. After we cross Water Street, we turn right, and . . ."

"No, left," Mr. Bauermann corrected.

"Where the construction work is?" I asked doubtfully.

"The construction work is further down," Mr. Bauermann answered. "We turn right as soon as we cross. I mean, after we cross and turn left, we cross again and turn right. Oh, the heck with it. I can tell you at the curb stops as we go along."

My source of information had dried up, but with the addition of his correction, I thought I now had my orientation straight and was mentally going over it once more, when Mr. Bauermann interrupted my thoughts.

"That construction work reminds me of a funny thing that happened to me once," he said reminiscently. "I'm big, as you know, and my last dog, Baron—I guess I just naturally run to aristocracy—was big, too. He weighed nearly a hundred and thirty pounds when he got old. Together, we totaled over three fifty. We walked at a pretty good clip, too. Well, anyway, one day we were going down the street, and this bird was up on a ladder, fixing an electric sign or something, I don't know." Here, Mr. Bauermann's infectious chuckle began to punctuate the narrative, and despite my more serious preoccupations, I couldn't help joining in. "Somehow, he spotted me and Baron coming along, all three hundred and fifty pounds of us, right for his ladder, and I guess it looked pretty flimsy compared to us. This fella figured he was done for unless something stopped us, but all he could do was holler. 'Hey, blind man,' he hollered, 'Hey, blind man!'"

As he laughed, Mr. Bauermann appeared very near the verge of total disintegration, and I found myself giggling inanely.

"Did you hit the ladder?" I asked.

"No, no," he gasped. "We didn't even come close, but I can hear it yet. 'Hey, blind man! Hey, blind man!'"

For some time, we sat there, smiling in the warm December sunlight. But suddenly, Minnie rose and began to whimper eagerly. It was the sign that Mr. Northrup and the other students were approaching, and with them my anxiety returned immediately. As I stepped forward into the middle of the sidewalk and put Minnie at sit, my brain was racing: "Thirty paces . . . Water Street . . . slight diagonal to the right . . . high curb . . . turn left and cross again . . . turn right for three blocks . . . second has low . . ."

"All right, Mr. Putnam. You'll go first. Wait for each

other at the curbs, and alternate the lead. All set? Let's
go."

I braced myself, and picked up Minnie's harness handle.
"Minnie, forward!" I commanded, and we were off.

"Hey, blind man!" Mr. Bauermann called from the rear.

"Atta *good* girl, Minnie," I laughed and we pounded on
down the street.

* * *

We wove rapidly through the early morning crowd of
shoppers. I concentrated on keeping my left hand well
back with the wrist broken, while trying to let the rest of
my body relax in order to swing easily with Minnie's
lateral movements. We stopped very abruptly at the curb
on Water Street, and I teetered at the edge for a moment,
but did not slip over. I had only just righted myself and
adjusted my right foot on the edge, when I heard Mr.
Bauermann and Duchess pull even with me on the left.

"Your turn," I said.

"Duchess, forward!" came Mr. Bauermann's voice, and
I tried to follow the sound of his footsteps across the street,
in order to calculate the slight diagonal to the right. When
he had had time to gain the other curb, I followed with
Minnie. Halfway across, the lights apparently changed,
and a large truck on my left ground into low gear. I could
feel Minnie's alert watchfulness in the little movements of
the harness handle as she looked from side to side. The

truck roared behind us, and Minnie checked suddenly to avoid what, from the quiet hum of the motor, I judged to be a large passenger car.

"Atta *good* girl, Minnie!" I said. I was beginning to get the hang of these quick checks, and their quality, with the sudden release of the powerful forward tension, when properly felt, was as decisive as an unexpected body blow. I was proud of our mutual co-ordination in this instance, and I rewarded her warmly again as we started forward. We stopped and I found the high curb, but as soon as we had gained the sidewalk, Minnie, seeing the direction which Duchess had taken, pulled to the left without waiting for the command. We nearly bumped into a passer-by, but after a moment of confusion, we had reached the neighboring curb.

"Hopp, hopp, right, Minnie," I said, moving my hand in that direction and edging sideways along the curb. Since this was rounded, the attempt to cross too close to the intersection might have thrown off my direction, and without this precaution I might have headed Minnie, not for the opposite sidewalk, but diagonally into midstream of the traffic.

"Look out for Duchess," warned Mr. Bauermann on my right.

"O.K.," I said. "Now, it's my turn again. Minnie, forward!"

A car was pulled up to the curb with its motor running, and as Minnie's nose came even with the fumes of the exhaust pipe, she darted to the left, and I followed quickly. Again, I was pleased with myself, both because I had analyzed the cause of Minnie's movement, and because I had been able to follow it. On the opposite sidewalk, I made sure that we went forward two paces before making a right turn. Even so, I brushed my shoulder against another pedestrian.

Now, we were moving away from the center of Morristown, and, as we progressed, both the crowd and the traffic thinned. A blind man in the midst of sustained noise is in very much the same predicament as a normal person whose vision is blurred by too strong a light. He cannot distinguish one sound from another, and the sensitive discipline his hearing acquires greatly diminishes in value. At that time, my ability to recognize sounds was relatively undeveloped. Nevertheless, walking along this quiet block, my footsteps, echoing from the façade of buildings, parked cars, and trees enabled me to make some approximate estimate of their direction and distance. Minnie's movements, too, underwent a subtle change as she strained forward in a straight line on our unobstructed course. No longer distracted by the problems of traffic, I was again able to concentrate on keeping my left hand well back, while relaxing the rest of my body. I tried to swing my right hand freely, as Mr. Northrup had showed me. We sped over some rough cobblestone paving, and, after we had passed it, I began to wonder whether it had been one of the small side streets at which I should have stopped. Mr. Northrup did not break his silence, however, so I concluded it was only a driveway. Then, abruptly, Minnie stopped again. I located the edge of the pavement and listened to Mr. Bauermann hammering up behind me.

"How's it going?" I asked, when he came up.

"O.K.," he panted. "Duchess, forward!"

On the third block, as I again took the lead, I began to feel warm, and I removed my muffler with my right hand as we walked. I had never tried such an operation while in motion before, and I carefully planned each move in advance. It all went quite smoothly. I was congratulating myself on this feat, when I heard a sudden scuffle of feet ahead of me, followed by a low whisper. I alerted myself for a sudden movement from Minnie, but we went straight ahead without incident, and I wondered if Mr. Northrup had been up to something. When Mr. Bauermann joined me at the next curb, he was breathing heavily.

"O.K.?" I asked.

"Murder!" groaned Mr. Bauermann. "Duchess, you're killing me. All right, Duchess, left!"

He was off, and on this block, it was my turn to cry murder. It was a long one, and my muscles were beginning to stiffen up. Otherwise, everything went well, and Minnie led me smoothly around a small child on roller skates. In the meantime, my curiosity about the scuffling sound on the previous block had time to grow, and when I pulled up next to Mr. Bauermann, I turned around and addressed the space behind me.

"Mr. Northrup?" I called. "What happened up ahead of me at the end of the last block?"

The answer came from the middle of the street in front of me, and it was no answer, but its tone confirmed my suspicions. "All right, Mr. Putnam," the voice reproved. "Cross and turn left."

I shrugged my shoulders and gave Minnie the command. On the opposite side of the street, I encountered, not the expected curb, but the cement slope of a driveway at which Minnie neglected to stop. Thinking quickly, I dropped the harness handle, still holding Minnie by the leash and took one step back into the street, muttering a venomous "Quit it!"

"Minnie, come!" I said, jerking the leash slightly, and when she had circled around to my left side, I rewarded her and put her at sit. Then, I stamped on the edge of the driveway with my right foot.

"See that, Minerv?" I reproved. "When you come to that you're supposed to stop." Then, I picked up the harness again, and we were off.

"How was that?" I called over my shoulder to Mr. Northrup.

"I suppose you think you're pretty smart!" a voice muttered close to my ear, and I laughed.

The next block was a long one, beginning with a downgrade. Even though I was in the lead, Minnie pulled hard, and several times I tried the method Mr. Northrup had showed me for slowing her down, by suddenly releasing my hold on the harness handle and catching it again when she had stumbled. I was hot and tired by the time we reached the next stop, but now we were getting back into the business area, and the going would be slower. The curbs and turns became more frequent, and I soon lost track of the itinerary and had to ask Mr. Bauermann at each stop. Some distance from the dreaded construction work, the pneumatic drill stopped. It did not begin again until I was nearly on top of it. Minnie started slightly, but I nearly jumped a foot, and I was sure Mr. Northrup was laughing at me. Then, Minnie snaked daintily along a board walk which, I later learned, lay over a deep ditch, and we went on our way. At another place, we went through a narrow alley with nearly a score of steps at irregular intervals and, then, across several busy streets. Apart from being slightly distracted by a yelping mongrel, Minnie behaved herself admirably through the rest of the trip. I was tired, but we were both triumphant when we arrived again in front of the bus depot.

"I'm dying!" Mr. Bauermann groaned, sinking heavily to the bench. We had still a little wait for the return bus to the Seeing Eye, and, since the second shift of students had not yet arrived, Mr. Northrup joined us while we waited.

"Cigarette, Mr. Bauermann?" I asked, and when he had taken one, I turned to Mr. Northrup. "What really happened back there on the street?"

"You're a persistent cuss, aren't you?" Mr. Northrup countered sardonically. "Why should it concern *you*?"

"Well, I just thought that if I was going to bump into something, and you had to interfere, because I wasn't doing something right, I ought to know about it." This guise of the conscientious student was a mere mask for my naked curiosity, and I don't think it fooled Mr. Northrup for a minute, but he yielded.

"You were going to bump into something," he laughed. "A dear little old lady. She was about ninety, I think, and she was sweeping the sidewalk with her back to you. I got her out of the way just in time. If you'd hit her and knocked her down, and Gargantua here had steamed over her, I wouldn't have given a nickel for her life. The inhabitants of Morristown will put up with a lot, but organized manslaughter isn't in the rules."

"That's as bad as your fellow on the ladder," I said to Mr. Bauermann. "It gives me the creeps."

"No harm done," Mr. Northrup reassured, "and outside of that, it was a good trip."

I was very pleased, but before I could say anything, a heavy-duty motor ground to a stop behind us, and the hiss of air brakes and the roll and click of the automatic doors told me that the bus had arrived. The morning walk had come to an official end.

*   *   *

Back at the Seeing Eye, it was a shock to discover that it was only a little after ten o'clock. I had perhaps an hour and a half to wait until Mr. Northrup returned with the second shift. My activities during this time were pretty well limited by the bounds placed upon our movement. The desertion of the washroom offered a good opportunity to shave in privacy. For the same reason, my room, provided the maids had finished straightening up, would offer welcome seclusion for writing letters, and, if I were tired, I might doze for a half an hour in the reasonable assurance that Minnie, after her walk, would be content to leave me in peace. The Recreation Room offered the widest choice. There, I could assault the piano with "Drink to Me Only with Thine Eyes," study the large wooden relief map of Morristown which stood on a table in one corner, or puzzle at the mysteries of the little dots in my

Braille primer. I could converse with any classmates who felt so inclined, or listen to the radio, and, if I had received any mail that day, Miss Hutchinson would be up presently to read it to me there. To be sure, none of these alternatives was particularly stimulating, but, in my fatigue, I did not feel the stagnation of inactivity. Moreover, the mere absence of those anxious dissonances which had plagued me prior to the walk that morning was pleasant, and before I had really begun to know boredom, the slamming of the big front door below announced the return of the second shift.

Placing Minnie on bed chain, I went into the hall to wait for Mr. Northrup. As soon as he had put away the station wagon, he came up to us with the food pans. The dogs whimpered, whined, and eagerly clawed at the linoleum in their impatience. Minnie was a voracious eater, and, if I planned to wear a coat to the Park, I had barely time to put it on before she had finished. She used to nose the light aluminum pan across the floor until she reached the end of her bed chain and, then, preferring expediency to etiquette she would insert one huge paw to hold the pan firmly in place, while continuing to eat uninterruptedly around this hairy member until the last morsel had been devoured. Her speed enabled me to be one of the first across the hall into the lavatory, where I filled a bowl kept for that purpose with fresh water to wash down the meal, and I was then ready for the second trip to the Park.

Physically, of course, there had been no change in the yard since early morning, but the atmosphere was quite different. The sun was high now, and the air seemed surprisingly warm for December. The adjacent kennel runs, which had been silent in the early morning, were filled with younger dogs, being trained for subsequent classes, and these yelped enviously through the wire netting at their lordly seniors. A delivery truck, with idling motor, was parked at the kitchen entrance of the house, and the traffic hummed faintly on the Whippenny Road. There were other instructors moving about, too, and there were usually three or four students from both classes performing obedience with their dogs on the adjacent driveway. We were all more talkative now, and the pangs of a healthy appetite quickened my steps as I walked back with Minnie for lunch.

*   *   *

The conversation at lunch revealed the extent to which our work with the dogs dominated our whole horizon. The dining room pulsed with the same monomaniac enthusiasm which is to be found at golf clubs or ski lodges. The terms were different, but "Follow your dog" meant as much to us as "Keep your left arm straight" means to a golfer, and the corner of Market and South was as vivid in its connotations to a student at the Seeing Eye as the third turn of the Nosedive to a skier on Mount Mansfield. The elaborate post-mortems, the admissions of failure, the sympathetic cluckings, the reaffirmations of the determination to succeed were all the same, and doubtless the drift of the conversation would have been as unintelligible to the outsider. Notably absent, however, were those wild theories and stray bits of advice from one duffer to another which often undermine the efforts of conscientious golf professionals and ski instructors. All these were subject to censureship and correction by members of the staff who happened to be present, and their vigilance seemed never to relax. Even our most innocent remarks were occasionally used as the springboards for an indoctrination sermon. I clearly remember an occasion of my falling victim to one of these exemplary lectures.

I had just seated myself at lunch when Mr. Curtiss inquired how I had fared on the morning route.

"Fine!" I answered heartily, "Minnie's really getting good." And I glanced in Mr. Northrup's direction for the expected corroboration, but it was not forthcoming.

"Of course, the rest of the class knows better," he began, and, although he was sitting at the same table, he raised his voice to be heard throughout the dining room, "but, for Mr. Putnam's benefit, I will explain that it is not Minnie, but he himself who is getting better. Minnie was already perfect the day he got her, and any mistakes she has made since that time have been the fault of improper handling. Right now, I could put on a blindfold and get her to take me anywhere."

"What about the railroad station route?" Militia Dixie challenged maliciously. We had not yet taken the prescribed trip through the local station, much dreaded because of the absence of well-defined paths to channel our movements, the jostling haste of crowds of travelers, and the distracting clatter of incoming and outgoing trains, but its ill fame had been spread by the reports of the second timers.

"Well," Mr. Northrup answered with deliberate hesitancy, "I don't know about the railroad station. After all, we lose more than half our students there."

Amid the general outburst of laughter which followed, Mrs. Clay could be heard moaning: "Oh, dear, I wish Mr. Northrup wouldn't joke like that!"

* * *

The afternoon schedule was a repetition, in outline, of that of the morning, but my experience of it always differed slightly. The routes we traveled were rarely the same, and I was usually paired with a different walking companion. It was seldom that two walks on the same day met with equal success, but I was not oppressed by that nervous anxiety which had troubled my morning, and, for this very reason, perhaps, the ennui of the waiting period was more pronounced. The third trip to the Park, too, was different. We curried and brushed our dogs in the same driveway on which we had previously performed obedience. This was sheer ecstasy for Minerva. At first, I had been afraid that the steel teeth of the curry comb would abrade her skin, but I soon found that, with the exception of the bony protuberances at the shoulders and hips, the harder I massaged her back, the better she liked it. Later, at Princeton, the mere sound of the comb being drawn through the brush was enough to bring her trotting in from another room, and she betrayed a purely feminine vanity when her beauty bath was over, parading herself daintily, with mincing steps and gently waving tail, before any and all potential spectators in the vicinity.

It was not alone the fact that it signaled the end of the working day which distinguished this third Park outing from the others. The red orb of the sun hung low in the west, and the glare of its departing warmth on my face gave the illusion of light. Even unseen, the enchantment of approaching twilight made itself felt. The dropping of the wind, as the sun's rays warmed the upper atmosphere, imparted a certain softness to the quiet air. As I moved about the gravel yard through the silent element, I felt myself a peculiarly earthbound creature, a blind crab upon the sea bottom of the air ocean, yet endowed with a poignant consciousness of its limitless extent above and beyond. A dog was barking in the distance, an automobile horn sounded faintly, as though stirred, yet saddened, by the imminent invasion of night. An occasional sigh of the dying breeze wafted a breath of the chill collecting in the deepening shadows. These things brought sunset to my ears and to the exposed surface of my skin, as the constantly changing refractions of the dimming light bring it to the eye, and, walking back with Minnie over the familiar path to the big house, I was pervaded by a glow of anticipation for the coming of evening.

* * *

Before dinner, I took a leisurely shower. The lavatory was a narrow oblong, and I leashed Minnie to the sink trap of the janitor's basin at the far end next to a stall shower. The drumming of the water drowned my baritone imperfections and I enjoyed the resonance my voice acquired in the confined space. Occasionally, I paused in mid-song to assure Minnie, who was puzzled by all this splashing and roaring, that she was, in very truth, a good girl. Emerging at last, I retreated rapidly from the licking tongue eager for a salty taste of my warm hind. Dressing again in my room, I eavesdropped on the Recreation Room conversation. Mr. Torbak was making his habitual demand.

"Hey, McNeill, gat summ noose on de raddio!"

"Tobaccy must own stock in a munitions corporation,"

Mr. McNeill announced, and having switched on the radio, he prepared to leave the room to take his place at the head of the stairs. "It's a regular business with 'im. He don't miss a single war bulletin."

"Ya!" Mr. Torbak shouted after him. "And I notiss you dunt miss no meals neider!"

Dinner was a less boisterous meal than lunch. Our work was over, and there was no pressure to meet the afternoon schedule. At midday, the various members of the staff who did not live at the Seeing Eye were scattered as "guests" among the little tables. Their conversation was both pleasant and stimulating, but it tended to repress those personal reminiscences which gave me glimpses into the lives of my tablemates. For example, there was Mr. Curtiss' anecdote of the lady who had denied him admittance to tune her piano. "You can't bring that wolf in here!" she had shrieked and slammed the door. Militia Dixie had helped out in her aunt's general store the previous summer. With the unconscious cruelty of the young, the children had thought it a great joke to take pop bottles from the cooler, shake them violently, and ask her to open them.

"They'd fizz all ovah the floor an' sticky mah shews. It were a mess."

"The little bums," I said.

"Oh, they didden know no bettah," she said philosophically, and then smirked, "an' when I tol' em they wuz payin' fahve cents for half a bottle, they smartened up some."

Trivial as they were, these stories gave tangible details of lives widely different from my own, and the simple way they were told bespoke an acceptance of life which had nothing to do with resignation. Much as I enjoyed the conversation of my tablemates, Mr. Northrup's presence always added greatly to my own pleasure in the meal. I had grown to like him immensely, and I think he liked me too. When he was at our table, I lingered as long as I dared over coffee and cigarettes. He lived at the Seeing Eye on twenty-four-hour call (despite the fact that his wife was momentarily expecting their first child), but he was so constantly occupied with his duties that this was almost our sole opportunity for intimacy. With a certain sophomoric snobbishness I felt that our conversations had attained a rather high intellectual plane. I had discovered that he was currently absorbed in Nietzsche's *Thus Spake Zarathustra*, and twice he actually read aloud to me short passages whose meaning we afterward debated. When the clatter of the maids clearing away dinner dishes and setting up for breakfast could no longer be ignored, I reluctantly rubbed the end of my cigarette into the ash tray and resigned myself to the less "high-brow" entertainment of the Recreation Room.

With the exception of Mr. Torbak, who, when he was

not catching up on the "noose," spent most of his time in his bedroom, everyone was there. Our tastes in radio programs differed widely, games with Braille cards proved tedious, and, because of the diversity of the social elements we represented, even conversation was often difficult. Militia's singing was a happy solution. Her choice of songs made the most of her three-chord accompaniment, and her enthusiasm was contagious.

Mr. Ballard was particularly loud in his praises. In his shy way, I suspect he was rather drawn to Militia Dixie (whom he had never dared to address by this familiar title) and was miffed that Mr. Curtiss and I, as her tablemates, were thrown so much more in her company. As compensation, he exploited his wide acquaintance with the western, hillbilly, and other modern folk songs of her repertory to open conversations revealing a realm of music whose very existence I had not previously suspected. Its first lady was a certain "Sunbonnet Sue," and on hearing their eulogies, not only of her voice, but of her charm, beauty, and sweetness of disposition, it was impossible, notwithstanding the incredible pseudonym, to avoid a kind of vicarious adulation.

Occasionally we joined in the more familiar numbers. Mrs. Clay trilled the words in a wistful warble suggesting a nostalgic devotion to Helen Morgan, while Mr. Bauermann, in a bass which rendered the lyrics irrelevant, oom-phed an accompaniment beneath her. Sometimes, the students of the other class responded with a chorus from the Recreation Room on the other side of the stair well, and it was after one of these rival concerts one night that Mr. Torbak, emerging from his boudoir isolation, asked an unexpected question.

"Miss Bork!" he trumpeted.

"Yes, Mr. Torbak?" Militia responded politely. For all her breeziness, she was unfailingly mindful of the respect owing our senior member.

"Look out!" Mr. Ballard interrupted unceremoniously. "You nearly stepped on Emma."

Maneuvering around the prostrate dogs required some skill when the Recreation Room was full, and Mr. Torbak was not particularly adept. But he was not to be deterred from his mission, and, when he had shuffled his way to a seat, he resumed.

"Miss Bork, you know Seegma Chi?"

"You mean Omar Khayyam, don't ye, Tobaccy?" Mr. McNeill put in.

"No, no, Seegma Chi!" Mr. Torbak continued impatiently and then added, as if it explained everything, "Detsh Grik!"

"Come on now, Tobaccy," Mr. McNeill objected. "Miss Burke don't know no Greek songs."

"Detsh frottornity! 'Merracan, not Grik!" Mr. Torbak

fairly exploded. "My son belunks by univorsity. Dey got sonk!" He articulated the title laboriously, but with undiminished scorn. " 'Svittheart fon Seegma Chi.' "

"Well, well!" Mr. Northrup's voice sounded cordially from the doorway. He had come to tell us it was time for the last trip to the Park. "I belonged to the Duke chapter of Sigma Chi. It's a darned good fraternity, and a darned good song, too. Do you know it, Miss Burke?"

"See, McNeill!" Mr. Torbak roared triumphantly, but Miss Burke had already struck the opening chord, and Mr. Northrup was leading the chorus. Although we were a little uncertain of the lyrics, Mr. Curtiss and I got in some pretty good barber-shop stuff at the end, and we all applauded enthusiastically.

"Let's try it again," Mr. Northrup laughed. "It ain't good, but it's loud."

This time, the students of the other class could be heard through the ragged pauses of the chorus.

"All right," Mr. Northrup said, getting back to business. "Let's take the dogs down to the Park. If we keep this up, they'll be wetting all over the place."

We were all in good spirits. The night had turned very cold, and the dogs stood for long moments pointing their noses into the still winter moving down from the north, but, beneath the hushed surface of night, there seemed always ready to break through a warm current of laughter. Sinking at last into sleep, the many-voiced fugue of my day at the Seeing Eye ended. Anxiety, exertion, fatigue, ennui, isolation, laughter, camaraderie had played their parts, and that night the last strains to ebb from my waning consciousness were:

> The moonlight beams
> On the girl of my dreams.
> She's the sweetheart of Sigma Chi.

CHAPTER VI

The Monastery and the World

I HAD COME TO THE SEEING EYE OBSESSED WITH THE expectation that I must live for a month as a sort of human spore, in a state of suspended animation. In the beginning my ego, continually at war with a gnawing fear of ultimate failure, had built for me a hard defensive shell within which I dwelt isolated from all outside contacts. Gradually, however, my dawning confidence had lessened my nervous preoccupation with the moment, and I had been able to observe sympathetically the personalities and problems of my fellow students. My objective interest in the scientific aspects of guide-dog education had been another symptom of an outgoing consciousness. And, toward the end, I began to formulate something like a total impression of the Seeing Eye as an institution. The larger picture had to be pieced together from a series of seemingly disconnected little scenes, but my imagination gratuitously supplied a stream of continuity and three-dimensionality to the otherwise flat and disjointed images discernible from my "worm's eye view." The division of our day into many little parts left small opportunity for sustained social intercourse with the busy members of the staff, and for this reason I had only glimpses of them as fellow human beings through chinks in the armor of the daily routine. Rigorous as was the schedule, however, I found that the Seeing Eye staff seemed to have developed a knack for softening its strictures and humanizing its impersonality in the very act of fulfilling its requirements.

A typical instance of one of these human moments in the midst of the performance of duty is my most vivid recollection of Mr. Debetaz. He was a French Swiss whom Mr. Humphrey had trained for the post of chief instructor, and I know he must often have watched Minnie and me in our progress through the streets, but his duties rarely brought him in direct personal contact. One morning in Morristown, after we had completed our rounds, he opened the front door of the station wagon, parked in front of a drugstore where Mr. Northrup was making cigarette purchases for the class.

"Good morning, good morning," he said cheerfully, as he got in. "Today, I am an 'eetch-hikaire."

As usual, at this time, we students were discussing our most recent adventures with great animation, and the din of conversation was considerable.

"Quiet! Quiet!" shouted Mr. Debetaz. "A leetleh less noise in 'ere!"

He had scarcely uttered these words when a sharp report reverberated in the narrow confines of the closed station wagon. Mr. Debetaz had fired a large cap pistol. It was, apparently, a regular practice to test the poise of masters and dogs in the face of a sudden disturbance, but Mr. Debetaz's good-humored way of bringing it off lifted it above the level of mere routine.

The far more personal supervision of our immediate instructor, Mr. Northrup, displayed a similar tempering of regular business with a sort of good-natured horseplay. As a Duke alumnus, he frequently contrasted the merits of their great football team with the miserable record of the Princeton eleven. On the first Sunday on which he called me into the hall to give me Minnie's beef knuckle, he told me to stick out my finger. As I naïvely extended a stiffened digit, he pushed it into the cold slime of the marrow, laughing delightedly at my expression of disgust.

"That, Mr. Putnam," he announced, "is just about the consistency of the Tiger line."

On another occasion, I was crossing the driveway by the Park to return to the big house, when a car, idling on my left, suddenly zoomed forward. Minnie swerved sharply to the right, very nearly tripping me, and when I had regained my balance, we proceeded, according to my calculations, toward the house. Unknown to me, the strange car, like Mr. Debetaz's pistol shot, had been designed to test my presence of mind in an unsuspecting moment. Some twenty or thirty paces later,

I began to sense that something was wrong, and when I arrived before an unfamiliar doorway, I became convinced of it. After her turn to avoid the automobile ambush, Minnie, finding herself on the path to the kennels, had continued blithely onward in the apparent belief that she was returning to her old home. I was feeling of the doorway in some perplexity when a familiar voice rang out in the distance.

"Going back to Nassau Hall, Mr. Putnam?"

Whatever the merits of this sort of thing as repartee, it tended to add color and warmth to the performance of routine duties.

Other moments in my acquaintance with Mr. Northrup held a more personal meaning, establishing associations which often bring him into my mind apart from other recollections of the school. One evening at dinner I was eulogizing the character of the course at the Seeing Eye, comparing it to my experience in the Princeton Triangle Club, when he interrupted from another table.

"Easy on the chauvinism, Mr. Putnam," he called.

"What's chauvinism?" I asked.

He seemed momentarily embarrassed by the question, and I guessed that the word was new to him.

"Why, it's an exaggerated loyalty to a person or a thing," he said, hesitantly, "like extreme nationalism. Isn't it? You ought to know. You're a Princeton man."

"I guess that's a word they were saving for my senior

year," I said. I was pleased at the hint of the intellectual intimacy which might be expected to subsist between us.

My vanity was further flattered on the following Saturday, when I collaborated in his conspiracy to hasten the afternoon outing to the Park in order to gain time to hear the broadcast of the last act of *Die Walküre*.

Since the musical tastes of the Recreation Room never rose much above the level of "The Sweetheart of Sigma Chi," he permitted me to join him in his bedroom, normally considered as "off bounds" for us students. He was unfamiliar with the Ring legend, and I found it very pleasant, after two weeks, to be dispensing information to my teacher. Afterward, warmed by the music, I lingered for some time in conversation, and it was then that he first read me snatches of *Thus Spake Zarathustra*. All in all, I came away wishing that I might have had his permanent friendship and saddened at the thought that our association would end with my departure from the Seeing Eye.

* * *

I saw little of Miss Hutchinson except when she read me my mail, but as many members of my family wrote to me frequently, we sat alone in the Recreation Room almost daily. I should judge she was about thirty at the time and the sort of woman who could be taken for thirty ten years later. She read with a clear well-modulated voice, and I was impressed at the ease with which she mastered the script of two correspondents whose letters had often caused me some difficulty to decipher even after long experience. Without prying, she took an interest in the letters and knew the names and relationships of my family in a short time. I remember her most clearly for her reactions to a letter from a girl who invited me for a weekend at a ski resort.

"Now, there's an idea," I remarked sardonically. "Can you imagine Minnie and me on skis?"

Miss Hutchinson laughed, too, but added reflectively: "Oh, I don't know. Maybe you ought to try it."

To a member of the Seeing Eye staff, nothing was impossible. Later that same winter, I did try it, and I found she was right. Ever since, skiing has been a source of much enjoyment, and I often wonder whether I ever should have discovered it had not Miss Hutchinson shaken my incredulity that morning.

*   *   *

Morris Frank, the owner of the first Seeing Eye dog, had been on a lecture tour when I first arrived at Morristown, but he returned to the school about a week before my departure. I met him in the dining room, but my first real remembrance of him is associated with one of the mail readings in the Recreation Room.

"Are you busy, Liz?" a fresh voice called from the hall.

"We've just finished," Miss Hutchinson answered. "What is it?"

Mr. Frank burst into the room.

"What do you think of it?" There was a display of pride in his accent.

"Let's have a look. Turn around." There was a short pause as Mr. Frank paraded himself. "Well, it fits all right, but," Miss Hutchinson concluded decisively, "the material is awful."

Undismayed at this verdict, Mr. Frank addressed me cheerfully. "It's a new sport coat, Mr. Putnam. I always have to get Miss Hutchinson's approval for my clothes, but I never do. This one's too snappy for her."

"Snappy!" Miss Hutchinson's voice was incredulous. "It makes you look like a race-track tout."

Mr. Frank laughed again and went out. After that, I often met him in the dining room. He had a seemingly endless store of anecdotes, gathered in his travels over the country. Once I remarked on having heard him lecture at The Hill School.

"Did you go to *The* Hill?" he asked, purposely accenting the article which is customarily, if rather absurdly, incorporated in the school's official title.

"That's no worse than *The* Seeing Eye," I countered.

"*Touché*, Mr. Putnam," he chuckled. "But I'm sore at you anyway. I'm sore at anybody who went to *The* Hill."

"Why?" I asked.

"Well, every year they give us a hundred dollars. . . ."

"That doesn't sound so bad," I put in.

"Now, shut up, will you, until I tell my story?" Mr. Frank breezed on. "As I was saying, before I was so rudely interrupted, the students contribute a hundred dollars every year, and I used to go down and give them a little talk. One year, I was pretty well tied up with some other business. I don't remember just what it was, but anyway I called them up and talked to the boy that was in charge.

" 'Look here,' I said. 'I'm awfully busy right now, and you're probably getting sick of hearing the same old line year after year, so what do you say we call the lecture off this year?'

"Well, there was a long pause, and for a minute I thought the phone had gone dead, and then this voice said, 'Look, Mr. Frank, we've got a hundred dollars for you down here. If you want it, come down and get it!' "

Mr. Frank was the first to laugh at his own story, and concluded, "So after that, I never argue with them any more. I just go down and get it."

It wasn't such a very funny story, but Mr. Frank's amusement was both infectious and genuine. Yet I knew that the full day's journey to The Hill could not pay for more than a tenth part of a single dog.

* * *

Like a corporation in the original and literal sense of that word, the Seeing Eye seemed to possess a sort of organic unity co-ordinating each of its separate members with the whole, but the man who appeared to me to have the most to do with the formation of its general policy was William Ebeling. German-born, he had been with the school since its inception, and, as the executive vice-president, he occupied the main office in the big house. He still spoke with a slight accent, and his manner was both cordial and reserved, but, when he spoke of the Seeing Eye, his tone assumed a special quality. Through a superficial embarrassed joviality, I sensed a deep seriousness, as if the words he was choosing were being carefully screened through an intellect which had spent many years in testing its convictions about the institution to which he had devoted so much of his life. When he lunched at our table, I felt an almost irresistible temptation to ask question after question.

"I must sound to you like a prosecuting attorney," I told him one day at the end of the meal. "I guess I'd better be on my way and leave you in peace."

"No, no, Mr. Putnam," he reassured me. "Don't worry yourself. If you would learn, you must ask questions, and a little conversation is good for the digestion. Come, you have time for another cup of coffee before you and your Minnie return to the stern call of duty."

The whole reply was characteristic—cordial, a little formal, and both mindful and reminding of the serious reason for our being there. I noted the implied admonition, but accepted his invitation and lit another cigarette, encouraged by his friendliness to ask still another question. It was one I had been pondering in eager daydreams for some time.

"I wonder," I ventured, "if there are any possibilities for future expansion."

"Eventually," he said in his cautiously sifting tone, "we may expand somewhat. In time, perhaps, we may even double our present capacity."

"No more than that?" I was disappointed. I knew that the demand for guides was much greater than the Seeing Eye could supply, and that even former students, who enjoyed top priority, sometimes had to wait months to obtain replacements.

"No, I think not. We are not equipped to handle more."

"Couldn't you get the money?" I asked. "As soon as I've made my millions, you can throw out the Minerva S. Putnam Memorial Wing."

"Ja, ja," Mr. Ebeling laughed. "Good! The Minerva Putnam Memorial Wing is good." He paused to light a cigarette. "But there is more than just money to our problem. It is not easy to find and train our instructors, and we cannot operate here as a factory. Our task is too delicate, don't y'know?"

This "don't y'know?" was a frequent speech mannerism with him, and occasionally, as here, I felt it to be signifi-

cant. It seemed to indicate a certain reticence—not a rebuff
to my suggestions, but an indication that his mind, buoyed
by his superior experience, was drifting in another direction, and, as had happened before, the current of his
thoughts seemed to draw mine after them. I realized that
my answer was only putting into words the idea which he
had already implied.

"I think I see," I said. "You wouldn't want to lose your
. . . your *Stimmung*."

I regarded the use of this German word to a native
as something of a conversational triumph, and Mr. Ebeling
was tactful enough to accept it as such.

"Ha, ha! *Stimmung*! That's right, Mr. Putnam," he
laughed, seeming almost relieved that I had grasped his
notion without further prompting. "*Stimmung* is right.
You know," he continued, suddenly turning so jovially
confidential that I knew he was profoundly serious at
bottom, "we are here simply conservatives. We have found
something in this place, and we just want to hang onto it
. . . tight." I pictured him gesturing a grip with his fist.
When he resumed speaking, his tone had relaxed. "If the
demand for these dogs is to be met, there will have to be
other places like ours. Already there have been attempts
with some success, and so—" his chair scraped slightly as
he prepared to go—"when you have presented us with
your millions, we will take as much as we can use and you

may donate the rest in behalf of our competitors. That way, we can preserve our atmosphere . . . our *Stimmung,* as you call it."

The conversation was closed, and, excusing himself, Mr. Ebeling returned to his office, but not, I thought, before I had had some glimpse into the counsels which reigned there and throughout the other offices of the Seeing Eye.

* * *

The days, one by one, slipped by almost imperceptibly, for time had not its ordinary value in that modern cloister. Our mental as well as physical existence was hermetically sealed against any intrusion from the outside world, yet it passed pleasantly. My work kept mind and body busy, but, as I progressed, my walks with Minnie had less the quality of a grim struggle than the absorbing challenge of a game of skill. Through it all, my chauvinism grew. Only thirteen days had elapsed since my arrival, but human time is not to be measured by the calendar, and I had come a long road by the end of my second week. I had not begrudged the monastic solitude of those early days. I had rather embraced it as a means of focusing all my faculties upon the task at hand. By the second Saturday, however, I stood ready to welcome an intrusion from the world I had so recently and so long ago left behind me. That was the afternoon on which Mr. Northrup and I had listened to *Die Walküre* together. In the conversation afterward,

I had hinted at the anxieties which had so oppressed me upon my arrival. I can only partly recall his comment. It was something to the effect that I was making a fine adjustment and that "we all admire and respect you for it." On their first casual utterance, these words were lightly carried downstream on the current of the conversation, but, later, they recurred to my mind repeatedly. In the drumming of the shower before dinner, in the quiet of my bedroom as I dressed, and in the clatter of the dining room itself, they took form as the first concrete promise of success in the immediate future. And for the first time it was possible to look beyond the confines of the school grounds, beyond the bus depot, beyond the railroad station route itself, to the more distant future stretching toward Princeton, graduation, and the misty shapes of the life to come.

A ring on the phone in the hall outside the Recreation Room brought a more immediate contact with the outside world. It was a call I had half been expecting from Dick Sayer at Princeton. Visitors were permitted us for the first time on the following afternoon, and his cheerful voice informed me that he, Sandy, and Ben had been able to commandeer an automobile for the drive to Morristown.

"We'll smuggle you in a beer," he concluded.

"Watch out for the plain-clothes men at the door," I said, and we hung up.

A few minutes later we took our dogs for their last

airing, and when we returned I decided to go directly to bed. I was pleasantly tired, and the bed felt comfortable, but I found it hard to go to sleep. I listened alternately to the remembered strains of "Wotan's Farewell" and to the present sounds of Minnie's measured breathing and my thoughts were not confined within the walls of a small institution for the blind, but roved far across the surface of the whirling planet in whose darkened shadow I lay. I'd come a long way in two weeks I thought. I wondered whether the boys would notice the change.

* * *

There were no trips into Morristown on Sunday, but I kept myself busy in the morning catching up on my correspondence. My immediate family was too far away to visit, but they had written to me frequently and there was a considerable backlog of mail to answer. After the midday outing in the Park, I took a shower, shaved, and dressed meticulously, selecting all my favorite clothes, including the argyle socks and foulard tie I had set apart on one side of my dresser drawer. In the six months I had been blind, I had bought nothing new, and I still remembered every article of my wardrobe distinctly. It was pleasant to be dressing for an occasion again. When I came down for Sunday dinner, Mr. Northrup whistled.

"It's a pity you can't see Mr. Putnam," he told the class. "He must be expecting at least a fiancée this afternoon."

"Two or three of them," I answered. "Do you think they'll like my tie?"

When dinner was over, I had still some time to wait, and I decided to go back to my room to shine my shoes. I knew this to be unnecessary as I had shined them only the day before, but subconsciously I was drawing away from the society of my classmates, and it was a way of keeping my hands busy and my thoughts private.

"Still at it?" came Mr. Northrup's voice from the door. "This must be some girl you're expecting."

"It's nothing," I said. "We Princeton men are very discriminating dressers. They're not here yet are they?"

"No, but I want to show you how to introduce Minnie to strangers. Harness her up, and put her at sit." I buckled on Minnie's harness and straightened up, facing him.

"Peter, darling," Mr. Northrup piped in a high falsetto. "You look, but deevine!"

"No use of first names between students and instructors," I quoted Mr. Humphrey.

"All right, *Mister* Putnam," he said. "Now, when you've got your dog at sit, you hold out your hand to your friend with the palm downward. . . . That's right, and he puts his hand on top of yours, like this. . . . Then you put your hand on Minnie's head. O.K. . . . And, then, you take your hand away, and he keeps his hand there and strokes her a couple of times—strokes, not pats. Dogs don't like people to pound on their craniums. A couple of strokes is enough. The idea is to make sure the dog will be friendly, but if anything Minnie's already too friendly. Patting or playing with strangers will distract her, and you'll want to discourage it when you leave here."

He left, and I sat down on the bed. I had slept restlessly the night before, and I decided to stretch out for a few minutes. The radio in the Recreation Room was just opposite the head of my bed, and the music it played was soothing. Without meaning to, I dozed, and Mr. Northrup had to wake me when he came to tell me that my visitors had arrived.

"Is it the boys?" I asked groggily.

"No, not yet. An older man and a girl . . . his daughter, I think."

"Oh," I said. "That must be my uncle and cousin from Plainfield. They said they might come over. Gee, I hope the boys don't arrive while they're here."

I straightened my tie and then directed Minnie to the head of the stairs. I descended in my most professional manner and turned right into the waiting room where, only three weeks before, my mother and I had waited to interview Mrs. Campbell. Just inside the door, I put Minnie at sit. My cousin flung herself on my neck enthusiastically while my uncle pumped my hand. I was suddenly very glad to see them, but I could not neglect my duty.

"Just a minute!" I laughed. "I have to introduce you to Minerva formally."

The performance of this ceremony damped the warmth of our first greeting, and we sat down a little embarrassed on a large sofa.

"This is a very nice room," my uncle suggested rather tentatively.

"It seems to be," I said, "but we don't get to use it except when we have visitors. When we're not working or eating, we're supposed to stay upstairs."

"Gee, Minnie's a beaut," my cousin launched forth. "She's got the most beautiful eyes . . . and such an unusual color. She's almost white."

"Really?" I was surprised. "I had no idea. The official description they gave me was fawn color." Suddenly, I remembered Mr. Northrup calling her, "a beautiful blonde bitch."

"She seems lighter than fawn to me . . . sort of creamy, mostly, but darker along the spine, and the tips of her ears are almost café-au-lait."

I was feeling disembodied in this conversation, but my interests had been so specialized for the past two weeks that I could think of nothing much to say.

"She's a peach of a dog, all right," my uncle agreed. "I wonder, though, if that color might not be sort of a drawback. I mean, it's so unusual that drivers might not realize she was a Seeing Eye dog." This suggestion opposed the whole trend of my indoctrination, and I was about to explain that Seeing Eye dogs did not depend upon the drivers of automobiles for the safety of their masters, when I realized that my uncle was still speaking. "Did you hear the news?"

"No, what news?" I asked, expecting some family gossip.

"We heard it on the radio in the car driving over. The Japs bombed our naval vessels in Pearl Harbor this morning, and it seems that some of them sank."

"Well, I'll be darned," I said slowly. I had never heard of Pearl Harbor before and did not know where it was. I was thinking in terms of the Panay incident. "What were they, gunboats?"

"Bigger than that," my uncle said, and I was now aware of the gravity in his voice. "The reports are confused, but it seems to mean war."

The conversation continued largely by instinct, and I cannot think what we went on to say. The memory of Pearl Harbor has accumulated such a complex of associations and overtones through the years that to recall the first news of it, stripped of all later consequences, is to stare with mute wonder at the tiny splinter which the doctor has just extracted from the heart of a festering canker. At first, I felt nothing but a dim surprise. There flashed through my memory the vision of the giant head-line, WAR, printed in huge block letters, as I had seen it in movie shots of 1917. Mechanically I tried to estimate its effect upon my family. It would be a long war. My father might be made a general. In a couple of years, my brother would probably be in it, too. More vividly, I pictured my friends at Princeton, remembering that Dick, Sandy, and Ben were all enrolled in the R. O. T. C. But the first real pang I felt was at the thought that this news might prevent their anticipated visit. Slowly, at first, and then with gathering speed, the splinter was working its way into the flesh of my consciousness. Meanwhile, the unreal conversation continued.

When they had gone, I went back upstairs. Everyone was gathered in the Recreation Room to listen to the radio, but by five o'clock in the afternoon of December 7, 1941, the Seeing Eye was about as far as one could get from Pearl Harbor. With each succeeding announcement, the outside world seemed to be slipping away from us, and I, in my turn, was swiftly retreating from my fellow students. I was particularly irritated by Mr. Torbak's angry outbursts at "Dose yellow monkeys." "Be quiet, old blind man!" I wanted to say. "There's nothing *you* can do. Be quiet!"

The afternoon wore on, but there were no further visitors. When I tried to make a telephone call, there was a long wait before the operator answered. She told me that the circuits to Princeton were busy. "Never mind," I said, "cancel the call. . . ."

At dinner that night, I asked Mr. Northrup about his status. "I guess they'll continue my deferment for a while," he said moodily, "but I think I'd prefer to get into it." As we sat there, eating in silence, a great gulf yawned between us. . . .

In the Recreation Room that night, it was the same as in the afternoon, except that the voices of the radio announcers were pitched a note higher. I went to bed very early and found it solidly placed within its institutional retreat. The staccato accents of Walter Winchell, coming through the wall at the head of my bed, were like the sounds of distant battle cries penetrating the impregnable ramparts and cloistered stillness of a medieval monastery. . . .

*　*　*

On the following morning, we resumed our regular routine. The Park, breakfast, the trip to town, the walk with Minnie, the return trip, the feeding, and the second trip to the Park succeeded each other with the same soothing monotony. It was "business as usual," but at lunch a radio was moved into the dining room, so that we might all listen to President Roosevelt's war message to Congress. With the playing of "The Star-Spangled Banner," the chairs were scraped back, and everyone stood at attention.

The dogs were confused, and several got up, shaking their harnesses to go. In peremptory whispers, they were made to lie down again. From somewhere in my army background I thought I remembered that this was a violation of strict protocol according to which the audience stood only when in the actual presence of the band. In a word, my patriotic fervor fell somewhat short of chauvinism.

Mr. Ebeling sat at our table, and over coffee I asked him how he thought the war would affect the Seeing Eye.

"I do not think we will be much molested, for the present, at least." He spoke slowly, almost casually. "Our instructors have been getting six-months deferments, don't y'know? Of course, none of us knows what the future will hold, but I think we will go on just about as usual."

At this distance in time, the words may appear almost trivial, but spoken as they were above the confused rumble of world war, they expressed a calm resolution which did much to steady my thinking. In the many intervals of leisure which followed, I tried to explore the implications of my experience in the new light of Pearl Harbor. Like some predatory bird, winging and soaring in ever-tightening concentric circles above its ultimate target, my mind hovered persistently about a conviction with which it sought to close. The Seeing Eye was not, after all, an isolated monastery, but an institution which maintained daily contacts with the world at large, with public officials in Washington, with private citizens throughout the nation, and with its graduates across the country. The war, as a process of industrial production, military organization, and strategic assault, would last only until it was concluded by a process of conquest and diplomatic negotiation, but one of its permanent and inevitable consequences would be the number of those blinded in its battlefields. Eventually, many of these would surely find their way to the Seeing Eye, and it was this certainty which enabled me to rebuild the bridge to the future which had suddenly crumbled on that Sunday afternoon.

What would be the experience of these blinded veterans at the school in Morristown? Would Mr. Humphrey force them to overcome their handicap through accepting its harsh realities? Would Mr. Northrup read them Nietzsche, Miss Hutchinson encourage them to ski, Mr. Frank infect them with his gift of laughter, and Mr. Ebeling reveal to them the significance of that indefinable atmosphere? Would they there feel the camaraderie which I had felt with my fellow classmates and glimpse the far more lasting loyalty and devotion which I had sensed in Minnie? Would these comprise the whole of their experience? I thought not. Stemming from them all would arise a loyalty, founded in gratitude to the institution and imposing the obligation to redeem in society the gift it had so freely given. With romantic impetuosity, I concluded that it would be impossible for any sentient human being to undergo the course at the Seeing Eye without bearing the marks of the living experience through all the conduct of his later life. It would be to him as a fixed star by which he might always reckon his present position and chart his future course.

Now, ten years later, I can smile at my youthful idealism in the exaltation of the moment, and sigh at the recognition of the fact that experience has often fallen short of the expectation, but I do not less respect the content of that moment. It had its share of truth.

* * *

In the meanwhile, the demands of the inexorable routine did not relax. We fed, aired, curried, and brushed our dogs. We performed obedience exercises. We rode into town, waited and walked, turned and stopped, rewarded and corrected. Never for an instant were we parted from our dogs, or from those primary concerns which allied them to us. The dreaded railroad station route came and, in half an hour, was a thing of the past. We took our dogs through revolving doors, into stores, up and down in elevators. Perhaps the greatest triumph was reserved for the day when Mr. Northrup drove us into Newark. Minnie led me over four blocks of its shopping center through the crowds of the Christmas rush, and only once did my shoulder brush against one of the passing pedestrians, whom she nudged away from in front of me with her nose. Never before in my life had I moved so quickly and easily through such a crush of humanity.

The Newark expedition took place at the beginning of the fourth week, and from that time the members of our class began to leave for home. As the other class had begun the course earlier, most of them had already departed, and the dining room seemed very quiet at meals. The Seeing Eye arranged for a "graduation picture" of our class in the driveway in front of the big house, and when Mr. Ballard punched out all our names and addresses in Braille, presenting each of us with a copy, it seemed likely we might form quite an alumni association. Mr. McNeill urged me to visit him in Chicago sometime. Many of us expressed our intention of writing, although, considering my ability to decipher Braille, this was a promise whose fulfilment augured no unmixed blessing. On Wednesday morning, Mr. Torbak, with a final exhortation to "Go to Brinnston" and "Gat adducashun," departed, and only the trio of novices was left. We felt deserted, but we were reasonably comfortable in the assurance that Mr. Northrup's dark hints of Christmas in the Recreation Room would not materialize. We were sitting there the following evening when he joined us.

"Well, I've got some news for you," he announced. "Mrs. Clay, we're going to keep you for another day or two, but the young fry can leave tomorrow. We've arranged for your train tickets, Miss Burke, and, as for you, Mr. Putnam, you can phone your family to pick you up any time after lunch."

"Hallelujah!" said Militia.

"It's too bad you have to go so soon," Mr. Northrup said sorrowfully. "I was going to read you *The Christmas Carol*."

"An' Ah can recahte 'The Naht befoah Chris'mus,'" Melish added.

"Bad off!" I said.

"Worried!" chimed in Mrs. Clay unexpectedly.

*　*　*

Militia's train left early the next morning, and I took my last walk with Mrs. Clay. As we sped around the now familiar high-school route, it was difficult to believe that, in less than eight hours, I would be back in the family living room in Litchfield with Minerva at my feet. It seemed hardly credible that the whole course had been packed into twenty-six days. Back at the Seeing Eye, I had begun packing my things, when Miss Hutchinson came to the door of the room.

"Mr. Ebeling would like to see you in his office for a moment, Mr. Putnam."

"Right away?" I asked.

"Don't look as if the dean had sent for you," she laughed. "He only wants to give you your diploma."

She left, and as soon as I had put on Minnie's leash and harness I followed. Entering the office, I found that Mr. Humphrey was with Mr. Ebeling.

"Am I interrupting?" I asked. "Miss Hutchinson said . . ."

"No, no," Mr. Ebeling called. "Sit down. Sit down."

"There's a chair right here," Mr. Humphrey said, slapping its arm with his hand. As I took my seat in it, I realized that this was the first time I had sat down to anything like a personal conversation with Mr. Humphrey.

"So you're going to leave us, Mr. Putnam?" Mr. Ebeling began kindly.

"Yes," I answered. "My father and mother are driving down to pick me up. His leave wasn't canceled after all. They'll be here about two."

"Good!" Mr. Ebeling approved. "Well, I'll see you at lunch, but now we've called you in for our 'official farewell,' don't y'know?" He laughed. "Did you enjoy your stay with us?"

"Very much," I said, and then repeated more warmly, "I enjoyed it very much."

"We make it a custom," Mr. Humphrey explained, "to ask every student for his reactions to the course. Is there anything you didn't like, any specific suggestion as to something we might change?"

"Well," I said slowly. My mind was working very rapidly. It was an embarrassing question, particularly coming from Mr. Humphrey, but he stated it with an urgency which made me want to describe my reactions as accurately as possible. "Nothing here turned out quite as I expected. I had a wonderful time."

Both of them laughed at this slip, and I flushed, but in the same moment I saw that it had given me my cue. Recalling the grim ordeal and cheerless psychological isolation for which I had braced myself, I smiled too.

"Well, that's true," I said. "When I came, I expected to have a terrible time. I was braced for a month in prison, but . . ."

"You found out we were human, after all?" Mr. Ebeling put in.

"Yes, but . . . Well, I don't suppose you'd want to change it. You have to overemphasize the toughness, I guess, because you can't afford to have people dropping out. I mean, you have all kinds of people coming here, and . . ." I was losing my way. It was difficult to explain the fault of which, at least until the night of my illumination by Mr. Torbak, I had considered Mr. Humphrey primarily guilty. "What I mean is, I kept expecting it to be so hard. There were lots of tough moments, of course, but I was afraid it was going to be much harder. I was sort of scared. More than I had to be, if you see what I mean."

Help came from an unexpected source.

"Yes," Mr. Humphrey said. "I think you've got something there." His voice was not matter of fact, but eager. "Thinking a thing is tough sometimes makes it tougher, and maybe we've overstated our case. We had a man here once . . ." Mr. Humphrey had apparently had a man at the Seeing Eye to illustrate anything. "You remember him, Willie . . . Johnson?"

"Yes, I remember," Mr. Ebeling answered softly.

"He took an awful dislike to me." Mr. Humphrey chuckled reminiscently. "I told him I was tough, you see, and that I wanted everything done just so. I suppose I scared him, and he kept looking for me to make trouble. It wasn't easy to straighten out."

I almost laughed out loud. I wished I had had nerve enough to say, "You had two men here you scared, Mr. Humphrey. You remember the other one? His name was Putnam." I didn't, but maybe I didn't have to. I shook hands warmly with Mr. Humphrey when the interview was over, and, as I went upstairs, I realized that my last lingering reservation about the Seeing Eye had been blasted.

* * *

The meal was a very quiet one. Mrs. Clay and I were the only remaining students, and, as there were to be no new classes until after Christmas, the staff was not under its usual pressure. I had a pleasant conversation with Mr. Ebeling and Mr. Northrup, but I can recall nothing of it. Mentally, I had already taken my departure.

Upstairs, Minnie watched with interest at the end of her chain as I finished my packing. Her curiosity very nearly cost her dear, when I absent-mindedly slammed shut a bottom drawer into which she had been eagerly sniffing. I carried my bags and typewriter down to the front porch, and, as my parents were due any minute, I decided to take Minnie out to the Park for the last time.

We strolled around the gravel area without having to worry about getting too close to the other dogs and students. The dogs in the kennel runs barked at us through the netting. The air was cold, but so still that I could feel the warmth of the sun on my face. It was a beautiful day, and I did not want to go back into the empty house. We lingered there for several minutes, while Minnie, shifting her direction with dainty little steps, sniffed the air, first on one side and then on the other.

"Say good-bye, Minerva," I told her. "We're going away, and you're going to be a college girl."

She waved her tail slowly at the sound of my voice, but still stood dreamily enjoying the fall sun. The sound of a car pulling into the driveway reached us clearly from the other side of the house, and we both turned to listen.

"That's it, Minerv," I said. I led her at heel to the boulder and replaced her harness. Then I picked up the handle.

"Minnie, forward!" I commanded, and we started toward the house.

"Atta *good* girl!" I said.

CHAPTER VII

Afterglow

IN TWENTY MINUTES, IT WAS ALL OVER. THE CAR WAS
rolling out of the drive, and Minnie, sitting erect between
my knees in the middle seat of the family station wagon,
was peering out at the familiar school grounds for the last
time. It was December 19, 1941.

I have tried to set down above my impressions of a vivid
personal experience. Mr. Ebeling has been kind enough to
check through my manuscript for the correctness of inci-
dental technical detail, and I feel reasonably confident that
I have recalled much of the dialogue nearly verbatim. Of
course, I have taken some liberties. The names and certain
features of my fellow students have been altered, and a
few high lights have been added. Moreover, the inevitable
progress of a decade has transformed many details of the
routine. Returning to the Seeing Eye in 1948 to get a
second dog, I discovered that it was no longer required to

memorize the itineraries of our daily trips and that we took very few bus rides to Morristown. There were only three lectures, and both Mr. Northrup and Mr. Humphrey had left the staff. These alterations do not much concern me here, however, for I have only been trying to describe the course as it was or, rather, as it seemed to be. Even if everything else had been exactly the same, I could not have repeated the experience, because, of course, I myself had changed.

Moreover, I have not tried to describe every aspect of the experience. As I suggested at the outset blindness is not, perhaps, so difficult as many people imagine, and I had been fortunate in that my blindness had come at an age when one is very little committed to life, and, therefore, adaptable to change. Nevertheless, the blow, although I did not fully recognize it at the time, had left its mental scars. Lacking the searing honesty of an F. Scott Fitzgerald or the psychological insight of a Feodor Dostoevski, I could do little more than hint at the spiritual proud flesh which sensitized and sometimes disfigured my inner life at that period. Yet perhaps the reader will catch an occasional glimpse between the lines, and I believe that, in general, I have spoken true.

In another important sense, I have not told all. To quote John O'Hara: "Our story never ends. You pull the pin out of a hand grenade, and in a few seconds it explodes, and men in a small area get killed and wounded. That makes bodies to be buried, hurt men to be treated. It makes widows and fatherless children and bereaved parents. It means pension machinery, and it makes for pacifism in some and for lasting hatred in others. Again, a man out of the danger area sees the carnage the grenade creates, and shoots himself in the foot. Another man had been standing there just before the thing went off, and thereafter he believes in God or in a rabbit's foot."

I began this chapter by saying it was over, but it was the course that was over, not the experience. In the months and years that followed, that was kept alive by my many ties with the Seeing Eye. For the first year, I was required to write Mr. Ebeling monthly to tell him how I was getting along, and I so enjoyed his answers to these reports that I maintained the practice long after it had ceased to be obligatory. There were occasional talks which I gave either to clubs or to audiences of volunteer workers for the Seeing Eye's annual fund-raising drive. There was the unhappy imbroglio with the S. P. C. A. and the tactful understanding which the Seeing Eye brought to bear upon the problem. And, above all, there was Minnie herself.

She became so much a part of me that it was almost as if she were a physical extension of my body, magically grafted to my left hand, and sharing in all my subsequent experience. She led me to all my classes at Princeton and escorted me on long weekend train rides to Northampton to visit my fiancée at Smith. She walked me across the platform in front of Nassau Hall to receive my diploma, and she watched from the back of the church during my marriage. She dozed through the long seminars at graduate school and sat through the terrible hours of the oral examination for my Master's degree. She observed the funeral of my father, and, less than three months later, waited patiently all through one rainy November night in the overheated corridor of a maternity ward for the birth of his namesake. Our last sharing was of a walk on a fine September afternoon in 1947 outside a veterinary hospital in Hopewell, New Jersey. She whimpered a feeble protest but licked my hand when I returned her to her cage next to the operating room. I could not have told all of so long a story.

It is only in schools or on journeys that our experiences seem to assume a definitive form with a beginning, a middle, and an end, which explains, perhaps, why we tend to view the years in college or the summers in Europe with a special sort of romantic nostalgia. Yet, through memory, even these clipped segments of time transcend their chronological limits, living again with new values acquired in later years. It has been so with my first visit to the Seeing Eye, and, because it was a profound experience, it has not merely lived, but grown in its significance. The reflections which have accompanied the writing of this story have often seemed to me like the ore dug from a new vein in an old mine, whose excavation can never be complete. Only if I had dug the last deposit from the bottom of the shaft and hammered each purified and refined piece into its proper shape and place in this story could the experience be truly said to be over. But this will never be, and so, for me at least, my first trip to the Seeing Eye will never end.